KOSHER TIME

MOSHE LYHOVITSKY

ISBN 978-0-615-24324-5

I dedicate this book to my wife Suzanne
for letting me spend my time writing, and keeping
our kids Zalman Mordechai and SoraRochul
occupied and inspired. For her tireless hours of proofing
and being a patient soundboard.
Special dedication to Hashem
for giving me enough sense to understand.

Yehuda Jacobs

Lakewood, N.J.

יהודה יעבקס

לייקוואד, נ.ד.

יג' י' הרב ר' משה לחוצקי שליט"א הכ'ד ואראית ע'ן'
חיבור על ע'ע'ל בריאת הכאן אסר מא"ב קבע א
דאת על ע'נין הי"ן ע"ה דאת תוריה"ן, שע'נ'א זאהק
לג כאה מצוה, מאזרות, צג והד"א ציו"ן'ם ה'ן
הכניה בזק "כבר ט'ים". אולם זא הטון, סרות, האריו'
ע'י"ן להחמיר ה'ל'ן כבא"י אצ הל'ב להחמיר ס8,8
מ'וכר ל'ן מבור ומוחתק,י 12 מכח י'ר' ל8 188 המאית'
ב' ל'ק עד'ר'ע'ג'ן' הארום'ם ל'ע'ר'ה'ק צא"ו, א'3/א מחחת
131 לבב צג'ן ו/נ'א אחת'ק,
א' לצאת הל'ן' בצה, לאאר ו 0'3 והב'ו'הת מכווה
צגול'צאת מ'ב'ורי לאור ו/ה'ב' ב'ה' כב'ם לצ'וו'ר ו/ל'ה'
באעב'ה' ל'ת מכחלון לת תל'צ"ו,
י'3/לר ' ע'קבש

CONTENTS

ACKNOWLEDGEMENTS

I acknowledge Rabbi Yehudah Jacobs for countless hours reading and listening. Being patient and counseling me in a way that would make sense to me, in order that I would be able to postulate my thoughts in proper order.

Professor Michel Kadar of George Washington University for his many hours trying to explain physics. To be able to decifer my thinking and point me to the right source.

Michael Valantino for his skillful editing job. A special ablity to be able to transform raw thoughts into quality text.

Chaya Yankover for her comments and suggestions while proofreading my work. She exhibited a great care of my structure preserving it, ever so slightly changing and asking questions which would lead to more coherent passages.

To my friends Elimeleh and Mendy Horowitz for their research assistance. Finding things that others wouldn't even think of connecting.

Jonathan Gullery for his patience and keen ability to understand when others wouldn't even have a clue.

My Mom and Dad for their support, financial, physical and simple encouragements.

INTRODUCTION

THROUGHOUT THE AGES, IN every corner of the world, people have tried to give meaning to time and to understand their own fleeting existence. Some cultures actually believed that some sort of divine being 'Time' constantly controlled time; they believed that the sun rose and set only if "The Ruler" willed it.

In ancient Egypt, society deified time. Aristotle of ancient Greece believed that time was expressed as an element of motion: an object in motion was represented by time; however, a stationary object had no time element at all. Scientists today measure time in different quantities, such as the speed of light, quantum movement, etc, however the concept of time is elusive. Some scientists propose that time is eternal, having no beginning and no end. Others say that time was created after "the Big Bang," the scientific theory of how the universe came into being. They speculate that time came from nothingness and they attribute this ideology to all of the laws that govern physical reality, as described in cosmology. These "Big Bang" supporters can't even envision life or any point of reference without space. They have no explanation what caused the 'singularity' to occur – what made all of matter to condense into a giant black hole, nor what made the instability inside to explode, or any notion of "what happened before."

In Jewish perception, time is a creation just like any other. It is a causative dimension of reality that allows Man's advancement, changes his destiny, and improves his personality traits. A great Jewish thinker wrote[1] "past is like not, future didn't come, present has disappeared" – where a person is trapped between two absolute zeros. The reality of this world from the perspective of a world where time has no effect does not exist. Physical things have no value; only emotional aptitude plays a role, and the amount of moral conviction sets creatures apart. Yet, in the physical world, where past and future are just layers that are placed

---

1   Abarbanel

one on top of the other, the soul is not palpable. Because of this, some believe the spiritual to be the driving force of their existence and it therefore dictates their choices, their thoughts and aspirations, not only their physical necessities or hormonal desires.

People sense time differently and their five senses can identify it only so far. To a couple that is falling in love, there is not enough time in a second to express their feelings towards one another. But to a couple who just underwent the consummation of their marriage before family and friends, the moment somehow transposes into eternity, taking on its own significance of becoming a family. Meanwhile, there are others who portray time as a perpetual bore because they have nothing purposeful with which to occupy it. To them, each actual moment feels everlasting. Lastly, there are those that cannot find a spare moment to breathe because they are caught up in the never-ending rat's race.

Although, generally, every human being matures biologically, other aspects of maturation depend on the self-induced circumstances of the specific individual. One can remain a child even at the age of fifty if one never has matured emotionally, nor taken upon himself any form of genuine responsibility, dedication, or goals in life, or even the perseverance to accomplish the goals he has set for himself. Living such a carefree life can result in unconstructive and often harmful consequences. On the other hand, even those who, upon coming of age, set for themselves goals based on societal expectations sometimes see that these goals become more elusive with every passing year.

Most of us see time as a coefficient product of mental aptitude and general development. The older we become, the more understandable the world becomes. As time passes, that comprehension becomes deeper and more refined. As we mature, our world becomes larger. Our frame of reference moves from the sole focus of our immediate surroundings onto our country, continent, planet, solar system, galaxy and, finally, the entirety of the universe. However, spiritual development remains nil. Is it because Western societies emancipated themselves from anything except loving themselves, and becoming selfish egotists? Such emancipated societies have no benchmarks for doing good deeds, or raising children worth talking about and not snickered at. These societies preach humanism, where nothing is mandatory and values are abstract. Most, in these societies, have forgotten how to blush or when to cry. Some of these philosophical quandaries of development/time can be explained with a deeper understanding of the spiritual interdependence.

Time does not stimulate all of creation equally; some forms of creation, like stars and galaxies follow their own cycles of aging. Stars mature, some reach supernova[1], imploding, creating black holes[2], and swallowing entire systems in their cataclysmic demise. Our sun has its own orbit of eleven years[3], and, as was recently discovered, its own path that it has to complete. Even though it takes the earth 365 1/4 days to complete its orbit around the sun, thus giving us seasons, the moon completes its orbit in 29 1/2 days giving us tides, and some creations on earth follow its cycle. Human beings, whose average lifespan reach seventy years[4], seem to follow a different pattern altogether.

In addition to birth, maturation and becoming a family unit, one of the chief goals of interpersonal relationships is leaving a mark on the generations. It takes a span of at least three generations, however, for a person to see, in hindsight, the full impact of his actions. Only then, can he ask the grand question: "Did I live up to my potential?" He can, then, look back and evaluate how he used his time. He will then know whether it merely revolved around his existence, while he squandered and undervalued it, or if he cherished each moment and used it to the best of his ability.

With proper use of time, we can bring peace and utopia, not only upon ourselves, but also on our families and society at large. Learning and understanding the crux of human frailties eliminates the barriers that prevent us from becoming an influential force. It is our duty to discover our potential and thereby utilize time to its fullest.

For the average man to be able to function to his fullest capacity, he can never have any doubt in his own ability and must have the vigor and commitment necessary for the greater good. He must be able to hone and attune all his character traits to a specific function. He must be able to focus completely on any problem at hand and use his full mental capacity, not merely ten percent. This 'superman' perfection of the human spirit and awareness translates itself into being sensitive to other people's pain; and being able to comfort and ease that pain in some way, whether with an encouraging word or a caring deed. By helping and perfecting another's potential, we cause time to move forward, perhaps even accelerating it.

According to Jewish lore, this was the ability of Adam, the first man. Because he was cast into "time" away from the Garden of Eden, Man's essence shifted from the exalted Garden to the meager physical earth, and it became his sustenance. His current physical reality forced him to become more human and more "normal," and, therefore, he was no longer on the same elevated level as at the beginning of his creation. The spiritual level of the Garden was separated from its physical counterpart, making its dwellers plain. Man's sense of reality was no longer transparent to time - his senses were dull, his existence, a struggle.

What each one of us has is an innate ability to persevere through hardships, to learn from mistakes, to heal and to mature. As we grow, we desire to learn as much as possible in order to develop our abilities to the greatest extent. Therefore, we find mentors from whom to learn or emulate. Despite this, however, it takes a great deal of time and many, many hurdles to advance the development of our abilities.

In Hebrew, the word for *travail* and *travel* is the same,

indicating that as one travels through life, hardships are part of the journey of maturing. The only way to mature is to overcome the tests of life and emerge victorious. G-d sends trials to each of us as a means of helping us excel and become greater - and character strengths are the tools to overcome these trials.

Sometimes we stumble through everyday events and do not know the why's or what's of those events, leaving us feeling overwhelmed. Yet, by simply preparing ahead and not being sloppy, emotional, or just withdrawn, we can accomplish not only the art of surviving, but the art of advancement. Most of humanity only perceives events and people at a superficial level. This form of blindness was inherited from Adam himself since his initial existence transcended time. Originally, Adam's skin, according to Hebrew etymology, was light and permeated everywhere. One could see things for what they actually were - their intricate purpose in creation was not obscured by their physicality. Only after the sin did Adam's skin turn into the ordinary texture with which we are all familiar. Interestingly, the Hebrew word for blind and skin are the same as light.

Human perception of beauty has also undergone changes throughout the millennia. To the stoic society of Greece, beauty somehow was merged between ethereal and physical. Even though the Greeks attributed human beauty to their deities, they also supported human-transcendent values of beauty. As a result of that blindness, we too, do not see genuine beauty. We merely see that what we desire to see. Beauty of an object can be perceived, however, not only on the surface, but on molecular level as well, through its proportionality and its perfect fit into the bigger scheme of things.

The Rabbis teach us that one has to make a blessing on the splendor of a beauty queen, indicating that there are the few extraordinary individuals in society who received a special attribute from Above causing them to stand out. Does the internal beauty of the soul cause that beauty to be utilized for G-d's glory? Does the animalistic drive allow that gift of beauty to transform into a cheap worthless plaything? Certainly, with time, that beauty can only shrivel up and die. Yet, our Rabbis claim that the woman's main purpose is to beautify her partner's life. Does that mean that the outward appearance brings one to a closer relationship with one's Creator or does it somehow enhance life and make it exquisite in unison?

The definition of time is dependent on which aspect of time and regarding which culture one attempts to define. It is the term that will give dimension to the abstract concept. Linguistically, time is a measurement of one moment to the next, or at least the rate at which one can measure time that is relevant to other actions of accomplishment - like getting from one place to another. This will describe the rate or distance per certain measurement of time.

We do not actually know what time means in the animal kingdom, but we do know that some animals behave differently when the moon is full or when at high tide. Some shed their coats seasonally. Until recently, roosters awoke at dawn and aroused the populace, and bears hibernated during the entire winter and awakened precisely when spring arrived. The time conception of the animal kingdom is rather limited, compared to a modern day executive. A dog's time is measured quite differently than that of a human being. It dies after approximately 14 years. A dog has no concept of time except the here and now. It does not know its birthday, has no kinship with its descendants, and feels no need to set any goals. A dog has no desire to graduate from a reputable university or become the CEO of a major corporation.

For the modern day human being, time might be measured very differently, depending on his motivation or goals. To some, accomplishing a goal may mean to be able to legally drink in a bar; to others, to graduate from a reputable college or university. Goals can range from becoming financially independent, owning property, or simply acquiring a driver's license. These milestones are fundamental to the yardstick of success and time.

In the same vein of thought, when one observes design of a craftsman one will see the craftsmanship and perhaps even the purpose, meaning, that one can perceive not simply the object's value, but its place in the rest of the process of the design. Historically, there were some cultures that achieved great things and went down in history as spawning the greatest inventors of their times. Then again, others cheapened human values and humanity by reversing the progression of human development as though they had never existed - or, even worse, devastating their surroundings by their acts.

To cultures, time is measured through periods of momentous points in history, like the Age of Renaissance, Period of Darkness, and The 300 Year War between England and France. Once in a while, it is measured through a glimpse of enlightenment, such as the signing of the Magna Carta, the Declaration of Independence, or the Monroe Doctrine. These yardsticks are fundamental to those who are part of Western Civilization, but they might be insignificant to others, like the natives of Peru or the Aborigines of Australia.

Egyptian dynasties were known to be involved in the advancement of different scientific discoveries and, according to some historians, had sailed all the way to the "New World" and had started the Mayan Civilization. Yet, in the annals of time and history, Egyptian dynasties go down as extreme despots who considered themselves gods and all others as their puppets or slaves. If Pharaoh was hit with leprosy, he had no compulsions in killing thousands of babies each day merely to dip in a fresh blood bath. Waging war with neighboring nations for the purpose of enslaving them or for the acquisition of their riches was the standard of most cultures until recent days. They failed to set a shining example of societal structure and order or even the basic idea of humanity, by succeeding in improving the lot of mankind by being progressive and utilizing time to its fullest. They did not teach their descendants to continue their missions in the world as achieving nations who improve the world around them.

Time is sometimes looked on as a causative thing because it is spurs change and creates history. Our consciousness is not the only thing that makes up our identity. The depth of our identity, which is constantly evolving and changing with time, is also shaped by the weight of those moments that enrich our lives and to which our attention is constantly drawn. We struggle with life's difficulties and do not realize that the precious element of time is slipping away with every moment, bringing us closer to an inevitable end[1]. If one asks a ninety year old what great accomplishments he realized in his lifetime, or if he could have, would he have painted the canvas of his life differently by acting better towards others, doing things another way, or perhaps walking a different route, he could arouse nostalgia which might highlight his unachieved lifetime goals. He might see that time has elapsed with no positive effect, or, even worse, he has accumulated many bitter regrets.

PART ONE

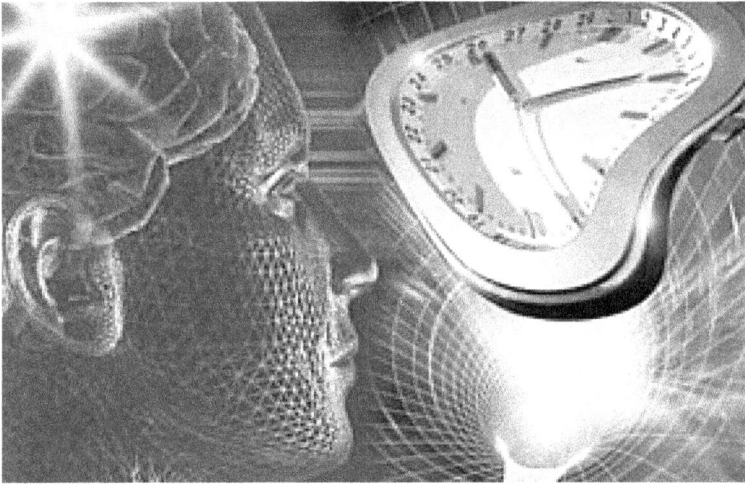

TIME

I RONICALLY, WE CONSISTENTLY TEACH children to "be on time," how to tell time, and how to count seconds ("one Mississippi, two Mississippi," and so on), but we, ourselves, are constantly losing our grip of time. How many times do we ask ourselves, "Where does the time slip by, where does it go?" As children, we read stories about people who had an opportunity to turn back time and do all the things they did not get to do when they were young. These fairy tales made everything sound so simple, but do we really know what time actually represents or its deeper meaning? Is it really possible to escape time's effects?

TIME AS A PROCESS OR A SKILL

S OME LOOK AT TIME as a process through which one acquires certain skills. Professionals of psychology will simply define time as a "process" of therapy. They say that it is the period that is required for a client to understand the broken level of reasoning, compared to the behavioral norm of a particular culture that brought him to his current state of being. The process is monitored to see if the client performs specified tasks of modification and gradually begins to relinquish those feelings. From this perspective, it could take the client years to accomplish a single task by ever-so-slowly working out all of the details that brought on that specific aspect of the disorder.

There are others who meditate or practice *Tai-chi*. The time becomes negligible compared to the effect of cognition or enlightenment that brings one to an alternate perspective of synergy. With every new nuance of the predetermined move, a new energy, on which the practitioner focuses and channels through any specific muscle group, slowly makes the force stronger, more palpable. Once the practitioner becomes engrossed and cognizant of every single move that the muscle groups produce, he senses and channels the energy, also known as, "*CHI*," actualizing it as a living force.

This perspective into once life is not yet achieved in therapy based upon analysis of the missing parts caused by depression needed to produce a new resolution or a much more global perception of the subject matter, be it *Tai-chi* or a psychological disorder.

HUMAN LINGUISTICS

M ANKIND HAS EVOLVED INTO having a full mastery of languages through many different stages of world history - from the Eliads, to Chaucer's infamous tales, to the Declaration of Independence. Words and their usage became our prosaic expression of our abstract thinking, and are able to stand the criticism of time and be relevant. Words, in any language, are references to the objects their usage defines or to the actions they perform. For example, the word "plow" is either a noun, meaning a tool that unearths the topsoil, or a verb, meaning an act of unearthing some-thing, be it snow, soil or the sea. Some words are concepts and also have specific meanings independent of their perspective or usage. The word 'mother' could either mean a biological parent, or a religious figure (in the ancient world it referred to a deity). This is dependent on by whom, to whom, or at what culture and at what time period the word is being expressed. For example, Eskimos have over 80 words for snow.

PART TWO

TIME

AS MENTIONED EARLIER, TIME is sometimes looked on as a causative entity because it spurs change and creates history. It has a germinating effect, allowing us to translate our dreams into reality. The people for whom time is measured moment to moment are the ones who go through life's hurdles while complaining that there is not enough time for everything they have to accomplish. They consistently wish for a couple of extra hours in a day to accomplish those endeavors. The achievements of these "go-getters" in life are hung on the mantel; time becomes measurable instead of being a process of internal growth. To them, life becomes synonymous with the amount of "stuff," materialistic accomplishments, and the quality of living afforded by them with which they can fill it. They become numb to other dimensions of life, like the preciousness of time itself. To them, the meaning of life, then, becomes only a measurement of achievement, conquest, dominance, and claiming a stake. They never really think of the consequences of their actions on those around them. However, there are others who measure time in generations, accumulating knowledge in order to transmit it to their descendants, and, paraphrasing Newton, "We are midgets sitting on the shoulders of giants." Perhaps there is a deeper meaning of time and perhaps life itself escapes most of us.

Interpersonal experiences make some of our perceptions of time invaluable and other moments unmemorable or even worth forgetting. Sometimes an experience of a special moment in time is so heavy, it is almost unbearable. Moments, such as when one proposes to a future spouse or when a new mother sees her infant for the first time are memories that seem to be engraved forever. They fill our canvas of life with brilliant and radiant colors and echoes for generations.

On the other extreme, a death of a loved one or any other extreme calamity could take ages to heal. The weight and the impact of that very important event makes the moment in one's life grow larger and take on a whole new dimension, never seen or felt before. It seizes one's attention and makes that moment last for an eternity, and possibly, even puts one's destiny in jeopardy. Necessary resolutions of the issues associated with that focal point of time are so epic, that it is as if no time is available for other events in one's life; nothing else can be implanted or developed. All other possibilities that could have occurred become inconsequential. Things and their importance begin to pale, awaiting proper resolution of the dominant problem. Life remains on hold. Our Rabbis connect this idea to a seeming play-on-words – *tuma/sotum* spiritual impurity/ being closed off.

Similarly, one can perceive this concept as being emotionally drained or numb, where the brain is simply set on autopilot without any proper cognition. Sometimes, in the course of dating, one gets a gnawing sense that something is amiss, that an emotion which was once generated by one party towards the other is still present, palpable and becoming cancerous. Those feelings take on a life of their own - haunting, suffocating.

TIME AS A GROWTH FACTOR

L ET US ANALYZE A meeting between two potential spouses, where one of them did not reciprocate the
emotions of the other or the one who rejected that prospec-
tive match moved on without providing any kind of closure
to the other. The rebuffed party might remain in a state of
utter rejection, thereby refusing all of the ensuing suggested
suitable matches because they do not measure up to the one
who said "no." That person begins to seek remedies, vainly
going to single's gatherings, and busying himself/herself with
a social life, yet he/she knows deep inside that the resolution
is not at hand. The rejected awaits that someone special who
could match the ego or the supposed values of 'beauty' of
inner soul possessed by the rejecter.

Meanwhile, all of the potential growth associated with
marriage is stunted and the development associated with
having a family is absent. The maturation process, which
was stunted by the circumstances of the original date, does
not progress; life stops, and with it time. The false sense of
ego does not relinquish control over the individual's over-
ripe sense of vision and things that are really not important
to the future make time stand still. The only way to resolve
the cancer of that haunting emotional ghost is to analyze
the circumstances of the stunted growth and perhaps allow

a new page in one's life-long odyssey to be written. This will enable the opportunity for love, family and self-growth to move forward.

Time causes our evolvement, progression and maturation. We glean things through learning and impress people whose attention we seek by making ourselves wholesome and complete. Consequently, if a person surrounds himself with pleasant and polite people and gets involved in a positive and productive communally policy-making group, like local tenants' associations, volunteer fire departments and/or neighborhood patrols, one will make life pleasurable through these positive interactions and environments. However, the moment the TV begins to cast its cynical position with all of its of 'colorful' allegories and 'murder mysteries', life takes on a whole different aspect.

In biblical grammar there is as a fascinating process, based on the prefix letter, called "*Vov Mehafeh*," which basically reverses the tense of the verb placed at the beginning of the sentence. "*Yomer*" translates as "and he said," even though "*Voymer*" literally means "he will say." This is because by adding the "*vov*," the tense of the verb is reversed from future to past. The explanation for this grammatical rule seems very kabalistic. It is to teach us that the past and the future are intertwined and depend on one another. There arc two distinct types of futures; those rooted in the past which come to full fruition in the future, and those that *flop*. Those futures that *flop* really had the potential to materialize into something special, yet due to some circumstances that didn't stand the test of time, fail and remain in the past without any future. The alternative, however, is when a potential future blossoms and develops into a time-span filled with success. The time takes on a germinating aspect as we impregnate it with our ideas, followed by our actions and expectations. We, ourselves, dictate our future, sometimes seizing certain opportunities given to us, developing and materializing them. Other times, we either ignore them or try, in vain, to develop them, thereby squandering and failing to utilize our time. We do not allow time, as an entity, to germinate those potentials.

Time plays a more important role in our lives than we often realize. The past and the future are in reality cause and effect. The action, or inaction, of human beings with a free will is what makes the difference when it comes to ultimate outcomes and germination of the future outcomes.

PSYCHOLOGICAL TOOLS

ANALYTICALLY, AN ABSTRACT APPROACH to time could shed a deeper perspective on it. By utilizing the tools of psychology, "Person In his Environment" (PIE), which abstractly defines a relationship and the circumstances of our daily milieu, we can examine another aspect of time. At the outset, we can examine a hypothetical case of a person placed in a cave for a certain amount of time. This individual will experience and appreciate the beauty of an instant; it evokes the feeling of time as an entity that slips away, like the sand in an hourglass. However, if we complicate the PIE relationship and examine the same person in the desert, it would lessen this sense, although it still would not be entirely absent. In this scenario, a person would be preoccupied with food and shelter from the elements, but would still be in touch with the inner sense of time and causality.

By applying this concept, a person can better his surroundings. One rarely comes to realize that behaving kindly towards another through developing this sense of elevated sensitivity, will affect his total perspective on life and causes others to reciprocate. His surroundings will become much more pleasant since like-minded individuals who do not perceive him as a challenge will surround him. Life will become full color, not drudgery and constant struggle.

The understanding of personal development as it relates to the societal rankings perhaps would be a better measurement of achievement and self-personification. Then again, an immoral society of cannibals would not be constructive, nor would it be considered the best of what humanity has to offer. Western societies today have no pressing need for spiritual elevation; they see no benchmarks for doing good deeds, and raising children worth talking about and not snickered at. Most, in these societies have, indeed, forgotten how to blush or when to cry.

Rarely does a person look at life as one's inner struggle to improve, or even from a deeper perspective, that incidental occurrences, such as a simple background noise, are needed to cause individual perseverance, betterment of the individual, and ultimately the universe at large. With the increased clamor of the modern world, we begin to lose the sense of time and cease to relate to each moment as a gift from above. Instead, we take it for granted - as something due to us. We become oblivious to change and settle for being merely mundane and average.

In humanity, the sense of objects and their objective value fizzles. Human relationships are perhaps the most complex, wrought with pitfalls of control, conquest, and other qualities that usually stem from selfishness and insecurity. There are many societies where values of betterment, kindness to the less fortunate, and mercy on less fortunate are not considered important. These societies glorify the "winners" and look down upon so-called losers, as their vision is merely skin deep. However, let us not forget that there are also societies that foster equal rights and equal access to those rights, and do not aim to spread misery equally.

Any society, in the final analysis, is no more or no less than the sum of its members. The concept that individuals are all nonetheless parts of one another, has deep roots in the Bible and in our common understanding of what it means to be human.

"THOU SHALL LOVE THY NEIGHBOR AS THYSELF"

THE BIBLICAL VERSE REFLECTS a simple, cohesive relationship in a society, which is one of the cornerstones of human relationship. People spend most of their lives attempting to get along with their peers. However, if one would put at least a minimal amount of thought into this statement, perhaps one would become aware of some gems of wisdom. Initially, one should consider why the Five Books of Moses state something so obvious. Secondly, why use the verb "love" and not "honor" (as is used when referring to the relationship one must have with a mother and father)? Thirdly, where do the wife and kids fit in?

The Talmud explains that one has to honor one's spouse more than oneself, based simply upon what is not said in the verses. An even deeper insight is learned from the incident involving a Roman officer who wanted to learn more about the Torah and its values. Initially he approached Shamai, one of the greatest sages of that time, asking him, "Teach me the Torah while I stand on one foot." Since the officer came a shortly before Shabbos, Shamai pushed him away. However, the officer was persistent and came to the sage Hillel, the other great authority at that time. Hillel answered him that the summary of the entire Torah is, "Do not do unto others what you would not want reciprocated," and the rest you can go and learn.

Hillel understood that the Roman officer was very serious about his pursuit of knowledge and becoming Jewish, and that his off-beat question, "on one foot," meant travel as when one walks one foot always remains on the ground. There are many questions that one can ask about that episode. Why did the Roman officer have such a great desire to become Jewish? Why was it so important for him to be answered before Shabbos? And so on. The basic answer was that the minimum required for stable relationships in a society, if it's members cannot accomplish the desired goal of loving, is not to hurt each other. The much deeper question begging to be asked here is: does one really know how to love oneself? Since egotistical people don't really love themselves, they drive everyone away, causing no love to be bestowed upon them and defeating the need to be loved. These people are ruining the Creator's master plan by negating one of the commandments *"Thou shall love thou neighbor as thyself"*. All of us have a tendency sometimes (maybe at most times) not to live according to these words.. To do so means to live differently, to shun the negative values of a society that is all too happy to ignore G-d's precepts.

PREDICTABILITY AND TIME

THE SCIENCE OF STATISTICS, which is so futile at predicting the future, determines certain mathematical progressions of economics. The concept of time, or time past, is not infallible since it deals with human emotion and ambition and does not just forecast a trend of some sort. Even though most people are optimists at heart and live their lives according to a thought-out plan, expecting things to generally improve with time, they are unable to predict the events of the following month, week or even day. To most, the events of the past seem to float naturally, one a result of the other, and in hindsight, one can always attribute a result on the effort that precedes it.

Yet, consider the consequences when a policeman stops a driver for speeding. He causes him to be late for an important appointment, which may make him feel unhappy for the next month. Thinking of this scenario, we might recall what happens to us each day. We remember all the little occurrences that just "happened" but do not comprehend why they happened. The hypothetical "could have beens" become muddled in our consciousness, gnawing at our brain, as if from some science fiction novel about a parallel universe where we had been the subjects of those events, and the "what ifs" become inescapable. The ideas of fate and religion become very preoccupying.

Many events that occur do not leave noticeable effects. Do they stick out, or are they in any way different from any other day of the past? If faced with this dilemma of past and future, one will wonder what is the true meaning of time – does it cause events, the passing moments, or moments have not yet come to pass? Do the façades of the external world through which the complexities or simplicities of time is sensed, or the effect that it produces really matter? does the social position of a person define him or give him any weight as far as his inner struggle to improve or to have effect on the external world. The interpersonal relationships that give us anguish or purpose, define us as feeling and being human . Each interchange with another person has great meaning, not only because we display our intellectual or interpersonal skills, but because of our ability to feel and improvise. They cause us to become genuine, compassionate - or simply passionate about life. Life will no longer be a giant bore and a pre-calculated endeavor. Does time give us ample insight into the world within and out? Time does indeed have powerful meaning in our lives, but only when our eyes are open to all of its possibilities. The choices that all face with every breath become more defined and obvious.

JEWISH SPLINTERS

IN JEWISH THOUGHT THERE is one gem that can shed some light on and explain reincarnation to some extent. It connects several concepts together. Depicting one's crossroad of life, not knowing which path will lead to success and which to failure, he may opt for the easier or more convenient path that initially seems to be the more logical choice. However, in reality, the more difficult path would have ultimately born sweeter fruit and greater accomplishment. In addition, in his next life, a person's soul splinters into smaller identities that carry the same characteristics as he possessed previously and he is faced, once again, with the same type of challenges that had not been surmounted in his previous life.

G-d causes those splinters to take a few routes and become separate identities so that the original soul can complete its previous spiritual growth and be able to accept even greater challenges. Once this is done, the soul will have attained what was required of it in that specific time period in order to move onto the multidimensional world. For some, it seems so simple to accomplish certain lifelong dreams, yet for others they are never-ending struggles. This explains why many thousand times more people populate the world now than five thousand years ago.

Time does not exist to waste on mere games, such as the rat race, where one strives for the finish line in order to become the winner. We do not realize that by filling life with meaningless pursuits that lead nowhere and bear no fruits of wisdom to oneself or others, we put our own purpose at stake[2]. Just as we learn in elementary school to read and write and interact with others, we learn basic things like patience, kindness and compassion from parental guidance (or lack of it) and our innate abilities. The strength of character we possess results in the friendship of others, and the ideas for which we are valued are acquired with time. Time is not measured by memories of past successful or unsuccessful relationships, but perhaps by the principles attained which instill in us accepted values. Time becomes nauseating for those who await something new and do not concentrate on things which are within their grasp to complete. They see those ships on the horizon that come for some and not for others - that new experience or that something extra - and blindly allow time to simply slip away as a wasted opportunity. Perhaps each one of us will act with deeper analysis and value the opportunity given to change our own world and the world around us. However the wasted opportunities are tragic indeed, as they are often lost forever.

DIFFERENT PERSPECTIVE ON HISTORY

HITLER TOOK CONTROL OF Germany by shenanigans and pure deceit. He then invoked emergency powers and started to consolidate his rule basically by sabotage or plain lies. Then Hitler started to create a myth about the Arian race[5] which connecting himself and the entire German race[6] to Persians by linking both nations[7] to the land and people of Assur or as he put it the god of ashur or athur or thur. He then assumed the biblical role of being Homon's descendent and criminalizing all Jews by trying to finish Homon's job of killing the entire Jewish race with his plot. He destroyed, ruined and devastated most of Europe and Russia and committed genocide on a global scale.

In 1946 during the Nuremburg trials the last of ten main

Nazi figures were condemned for their crimes. Ten major Nazi criminals were hung at Nüremburg on the holiday *Hoshana Raba*[8] in the year 5707 (1946). The holiday Hoshana Raba is traditionally the day that G-d begins to execute the judgments[9] he had sealed on *Yom Kippur* (Day of Judgment), particularly judgments concerning Jews. In every scroll of *Esther*[10], three letters are found that are small and one that is large. The three small letters *(zayin, taf, shin)* add up to the number 707, and the large one *(vav)* has the numerical value of six. They occur in a list of *Haman's* ten sons[11], whom Esther[12] had petitioned the King to hang - after they had been killed! The six represents the sixth millennium, the 5,000's on the Hebrew calendar - the 707 is the year, which happened to be the year the last Nazi got hung.

The last person to be hanged was not a military man and actually was forced out of power. Julius Streicher had created his party in 1921 and had produced the most virulent anti-Semitic diatribe ever written. Standing on the Gallows he screamed before his death, *"Purimspiel (Purim play) 1946!"* Perhaps he was hoping that Jews would mark that day as a new holiday and he would go down in infamy. Or perhaps he finally understood that he was a pawn of the Creator's greater plan to take vengeance on Homon and his descendents. Perhaps the world would learn the final lesson of who is in charge of the history.

In the last century lived Rav Nachman from Breslav[13], who presented a very unique way of looking at Jewish history. He wrote 13 fairy tales[14], which were full of colorful characters such as giants, dwarfs, princesses, and kings. In his introduction to the stories he said that these stories were meant for a generation when everyone will be asleep and the only way to arouse the listener from his outlook on life will be by telling these fairytales. All of his stories have one thing in common: a prince who has to find a princess and rescue her from her evil captors. it is understood that the prince represents the Messiah and the princess God's presence in this world, but the genius involved was to disguise different historic events throughout three millenniums with the usage of different allegory .

His view was that messiah is reincarnated in every generation attempting to succeed but sometimes due to historic events or the Jewish Nation lack of preparedness, he is prevented from accomplishing his lofty goal of uniting Jewish nation with Creator, bringing His presence amongst them. Rav Nachman perceived history as one unending stream of consciousness and every historic event is an introduction to the next one. Each of us has an opportunity to accomplish a certain act, even a minor one such as not stepping on someone's toe or treating a homeless cat humanely or monumental changes in one's life like being released from being jailed or worse, to become a prime example of goodness.

The Rabbi felt that inner insecurity or laziness (evil incli-nation) entraps all, from which people must break free in order to accomplish good things. Similarly, the period of Hitler was meant for some to act heroically and assist their brethren while others honor the Creator by dying as Jewish martyrs. Similar challenges may present themselves at any time during any of our lives, thus the meaning of "one reaps what one sows" becomes more clear. Will you be prepared for heroic action when some such situation comes to pres-ents itself ?

PART THREE

CULTURAL WAYS

THROUGHOUT THE MILLENNIA THERE have been different cultures that have come and gone. Some left promising traces and others... Let's just say we would have been better off if they weren't created. Cultures like that of Ghengis Khan and his horde, one of the most extreme examples around, ravaged from Mongolia through Russia decimating, killing, and maiming the populous. The Greek empire under Alexander the Great had a great dream of creating one large empire. They conquered all of the adjoining countries until the Indian Ocean and Hellenized all of them. Alexander's army was so preoccupied with conquering, collecting booty and proselytizing Greek ways, that the indigenous cultures were completely ignored and amalgamated.

SANCTITY OF TIME

S ANCTITY OF TIME IS a foreign concept in Western societies yet the word is used to identify a certain spiritual purity of the moment. One can ask how can time be considered pure, being only a concept. Time is a function of existence relevant to those that participate in its inclusion. But is there an existence beyond time and is it at all relevant to our conception of the world? Thousands of years ago there was a concept of wholeness which had measurements of holiness where sanctity was synonymous with purity of thought and cleanliness beyond immaculate. But with time, sanctity took on a different identity. To the Hebrews of two millenniums ago sanctity meant completely removed from ordinary and mundane, when connectedness with the holy was an everyday occurrence. People of that age were particular not to come in contact with death or any of its tangible ramifications.

In modern bioethics there is a concept of sanctity of life which seems misused or simply misapplied. If a patient is suffering a lethal condition, doctors will try to preserve the patient's life for as long as possible no matter how horrific the suffering. If the patient is lying undressed the doctor is obligated to preserve privacy and decency to preserve some sort of semblance of sanctity. Whereas the same person in real life might be scantily clad in a shopping mall.

Sanctity of life as most commonly used in today's society is very controversial. There are those who believe that a fetus has the same rights as any one of us, requiring preservation and defense. Others believe that a fetus that was delivered is a human, but while inside the woman it is relegated as her body; therefore she can do to it whatever she wishes. The concept of sanctity of the unborn and damages are Biblical. The narrative speaks about damages that one causes a pregnant woman and her unborn child, specifying the financial damages that the assailant has to pay, identifying there is a value to an unborn fetus. However, Rabbis postulate that the abortion is not sacrilege. In a situation where a woman is threatened by her unborn child, she has a full right and obligation to save herself by killing the fetus. The comparison that Rabbis use might seem unrelated to the untrained eye, but it is learned from the narrative regarding an assailant who digs a tunnel with the intention of robbing the house. Not only does the owner but any passerby has a full right to preemptively kill that thieve, even though the thief's intentions are not to harm anyone. Some rabbinical authorities will stretch this interpretation to a situation where a woman claims that her sanity is at stake.

Medical ethics has attempted to assign certain value to human organs that become available pertaining to who gets to utilize them. But if all factors are equal and the only factor that stands to ascertain is the value of one's life for another, i.e. if one of the competing patients is a nuclear scientist and the other one is a Down's Syndrome person, doctors very often make a humanistic decision rather than basing it on something more spiritual.

Sanctity of time has different meanings in different cultures; on Memorial Day we commemorate the valiant sacrifice that those before us gave in defense of our freedom. A wedding anniversary commemorates the focal point of the family, its formation. Those are different moments in time which are identified as sacred in different fashions, but sacredness and sanctity are not reflected. Rather, that is to treat time as simply not present and therefore all of the possibilities that stem from it irrelevant. For example, the Jewish faith dictates that with the advent of the Sabbath time stops for a 25 hour period and all the functions that were not yet completed are considered as though done. The mindset changes from being in need of feeling whole to a state of emancipation from daily humdrum.

Elections were resolved, business matters were complete, even cooking, carrying or thinking about certain aspects of life become mute, or none existent. A person transforms from a regular person to someone who invites the Creator into their life by abdicating all other activity in favor of seeing time standing still and life taking on a new sanctified meaning.

There are no parades, no confetti or party hats. Nobody gets gift bags to take home, yet the sanctity of family and of society is uplifted. On a superficial level one can answer that commemoration that every observant Jew has performed for Millennia is becoming free from slavery to Pharaoh, being his personal property. Yet this does not answer the profound meaning of sanctity that all of us have from that point onward. As every Friday night every Jew will answer "because during six days G-d was creating the universe and on the seventh He rested," in similitude we uplift time from a level of action to a level of going back to the source of creation, and seeing its purpose.

SCIENTISTS

SCIENTISTS CONSTANTLY MAINTAIN THAT their ideas or their schools of thought are superior to others because they follow pure intellect. Morality, humanity and humility, however, do not fit into that perfect ideology. During Aristotelian times, the Greeks used to throw their elders of the cliff, performing the politically correct euthanasia. During the Dark Ages, when the scientists of the time were preoccupied with making gold out of metals and the church was busy burning millions of heretics at the stake, millions of Jews were dislocated into ash; the fortunate ones were far away from Spain. Some attempted to save themselves by obliging the Inquisition, others became martyrs.

During World War II, Hitler and his scientists used to preach ethnic cleansing and purity of the Arian race by actively murdering millions of Jews and others deemed "unnecessary." Over forty million casualties suffered at the hands of the social scientists. Karl Marx and his utopian followers brought Russia to its knees. They destroyed the entire empire and reversed any kind of progress of the previous seventy years. All of these "scientists" brought demise to their theories and disgrace to themselves. They also turned around the progress of time.

G-d of the Bible clearly explained that it is a human obligation to be fruitful by designing, and progressing, and thereby making the world into a better place. It is humanity's responsibility to build up the world and populate it with those who will not destroy it based upon their own theories. Yet these thrill seekers of utopia have disgraced themselves, their followers, and their nations, humanity was disgraced with their presence in the annals of time.

There are countless examples of individuals – those who became great social, political and business leaders - who ultimately become disgraced, jailed for embezzlement, lies and theft. Plenty of leaders of the past millennium, such as Hitler, Lenin, Stalin, Pol Pot, Napoleon and so on, have been deposed, killed, imprisoned or have simply become a prime example of evil. Such individuals are perpetually self-serving, betray humanity, and even steal time from G-d. They reverse the time of progress, not only for themselves, but for entire generations.

True, these self serving individuals initially may achieve what is considered to be outwardly phenomenally important. Nevertheless, they do not deem it important enough to acquire certain basic moral qualities. Their perception of utopia is merely based upon their own meager comprehension of the human psyche, and they do not take into account the basic tendencies for good. These "heroes" are destined to failure because they use greed and power to rise to their positions and lack the pristine spiritual dimension to their personalities. As one esoteric statement of the rabbis puts it, with each consecutive appearance of Halley's Comet comes a new "ISM" for the consecutive world leader as a hurricane to lead to the 'Garden of Eden' only to mislead the rest to the false utopia.

ENMESHED FAMILIES

THERE IS A CONCEPT of enmeshed families that is taught in all Social Work schools. This concept began to be used during the 50s when welfare employees would come to check on single-family households to find if there was "A MAN IN THE HOUSE." They would stop by almost every other month in order to ascertain if there was a breadwinner in the family thereby removing such family from assistance lists. However, this welfare and those that sponsored it undermined entire generations from having a future. During the Great Depression of 1929 when the stock market crashed and with it the American economy, the government created a new concept of the WELFARE STATE: "public works," which began to give everyone jobs in order to build highways, buildup rural areas and so forth. This began to shrink the unemployment line and Hell's Kitchens, creating with it food stamps and all other types of public assistance. But it also created certain parts of society that solely relied on food stamps and public assistance. Single parent households began to be created with a design, not simply as a necessity. These families would band together to forge a new economic pact in raising children, babysitting for one another, share food and provide moral support. However, societal structure began to disappear.

In the Jewish Society there is a concept of Biblical proportion called "all of Israel is responsible for one another." Literally it is talking about an interest free loan with which one is supposed to back up his friend to help lift him out of poverty. But this design forces those that have, to take care of those that don't. Since those that get a blessing from Above have had that wealth bestowed upon them, the Grantor obligates the wealthy to use that money as a source of distribution to the less fortunate. Some families of today are known to have lines of people standing around the block daily distributing millions of dollars to those who simply come and ask. If a friend dies the entire city sends collections to make sure to take care of every need of that departed friend's family. May it be a purchase of a house, tuition or daily necessities.

During the previous century it was common for a great Rabbi to adopt lots of kids from unwed mothers in order to allow those mothers to have a fresh start at marriage. Those mothers would not have to worry about the stigma of being 'unwed mothers' or worse a "SCARLET WOMAN." In order to understand the depth of this concept one has to comprehend Kneset Israel/ Jewish Congregation.

In Jewish theology a person is looked on as a boat travelling through the sea of time. We are, individually, tiny boats, being swept up by the currents of time, wobbling, trying to connect to other boats of likeminded families.

In a broader sense, we can have the power associated with communities that connect with like-minded communities and become a prevailing fleet that can withstand the currents of ideologies that G-d puts into the heads of certain individuals. These would be people like Napoleon Bonaparte or Lenin who tried to sway us from the correct course. These hurricanes come to strengthen the inner bond between Jewish families to foster the concept of a Jewish congregation. If a group is traveling on a boat and one of the passengers is busy drilling a hole underneath him, he sabotages all aboard that ship. Similarly, if the captain is a crock or worse has no clue how to sail dangerous waters, he will be the captain of the Titanic. By becoming a grand Fleet we as a Jewish nation become the footstool for G-d, allowing Him to be the captain.

During this voyage some passengers might require medical assistance or food; those who have the capacity to provide take on those roles. These guarantors of the successful journey become not only employed by the captain but become part of the emissaries. The sooner each of us realizes our own role to play, and the need to participate as part of this great fleet, the better of we will be both as individuals and as a society as a whole in sailing into the future.

TV DINNER

H UMAN TIME-SAVING INVENTIONS HAVE not always proved to be productive in the long run. Yet, at the onset, they seem to convey so much promise in their efficiency. The invention of TV dinners signaled the new era of domestic bliss. It came at the dawn of the women's revolution, where women 'freedom fighters' were preaching freedom from family, child rearing and abolishment of the value system of that epoch. The aftermath of the Industrial Revolution brought the demise of a classic family structure, where 'Mom' was the provider of values and emotional warmth and 'Dad' was the breadwinner. In the end, 'Dad' typically was absent from the house and the majority of child rearing responsibilities, and 'Mom' ended up picking up the slack and doing double, if not triple shifts, in order to maintain a family. To resolve this inequality, the "freedom fighters" proposed abolishment of Mom's role and, instead, brought about the equality of women, where women were meant to achieve as much as men. This equality, however, lost sight of the family as a unit and of the family value system that was required to be transmitted over to the next generation. The TV dinner was meant to pick up the inadequacies left over by the new reform. It saved the time and energy of the housewives and gave them an opportunity to take care of their families without feeling guilty. They did not have to worry about having their kids wander to neighboring moms who perhaps showed more care or signs of domesticity by cooking their own dinners rather than running off somewhere and being busied with their egos without a care for that old concept called family.

TV dinners created a new kind of freedom. They created relief from hours spent in the kitchen and allowed new horizons in family values and a new sort of role model for women. The term 'Super-Mom' became the new ideal. There was no guilt and no responsibilities, freedom fighters were advocating, since the TV diner took care of everything. Mothers could go to work from nine to five, just like fathers. The house would be taken care of by cleaning ladies, and the children raised by babysitters (albeit bringing up toddlers speaking foreign languages). The woman's new reality began to take shape, and so did the modern day culture of single moms. Because of the lack of parental involvement in children's lives and MTV's new pop culture, kids did not even know what culture meant unless it was brought to them in a lyric or suggested to them by some great dance move demonstrated by the same "grand culture-gods of our *time*."

TV dinners continued something darker still in family dynamics and "family bliss" (dysfunction). Thanks to this wonderful invention, the household center of gravity has migrated from the dining room to the family room or den, or wherever the television is regally ensconced and enshrined as the surrogate parent, culture provider and false G-d that is to be worshiped at every spare hour. Every member of the "new and improved" family could now sit simultaneously on the sofa, eat dinner and be fed the normal modern-day-culture while *utilizing* time to its fullest.

The television discouraged interaction between family members. The only interval that a disastrous sort of quietude did not prevail was during the commercial breaks. Then, when the second TV arrived, the members of the family could eat in separate locations, bringing the total affect to its zenith. No one spoke anymore; the TV began to rule and dictate the culture. Some of the results were the apparent 60% divorce rate, single parenthood, a rise in teenage violence and crime, and gangs becoming the caretakers. And even though there was a lot of time-saving, and women definitely became more equal to men than ever before in regard to jobs and responsibilities, they also started encountering problems that came along with that new freedom - i.e. depression, alcoholism, violent crime, suicide and some other ills that came more to the forefront like bulimia and anorexia.

This was a classic case of good intentions gone bad. There were unforeseen consequences for this unprecedented tinkering with the mechanics of society. We continue to see the fallout from this mess to this very day.

COMPUTERS AND INTERNET

THE ADVANCEMENT OF COMPUTERS has set humanity to an added new level of the Industrial Revolution – something that has not been seen since the previous century. Computers have crept into our homes as fast as they made their way into every other aspect of modern life. We consistently yearn for the fastest and greatest machine to file our taxes, surf the Net, shop.

There is always a trade off to every comfort, however. Shoppers do not even bother going to the malls to get some exercise and parents hardly get to communicate with their kids, or for that matter, imbue in them their culture and heritage, because of the conveniences of the computer. Parents who work with computers see such instantaneous response from their programs that they begin to expect the same type of response from their wives and children. Some even wish that their kids would be more like machines - so orderly, quick and sharp. The speed of instant messaging began to ameliorate modern communication skills; writing and reading has gone to the level of the Ice Age. Words like "bling, lol, bff" have become encroached into our consciences. We are definitely proud of our time spending levels on the shut-them-up games!

The second reality (an Internet virtual life) has begun to

take over. No more relationships, no more real life. This new development does not bode well for humanity. Technology has yet again proven to be a two-edged sword, promising in its ability to help human beings, yet threatening in its potential to drive us even further apart, displacing genuine relationships with a vastly inferior impostor.

CULTURAL HOLOCAUST

THE SOLUTION OF THE "melting pot" seemed blissful to the early Twentieth-Century Americans. Hoping for a quick adaptation of the realities of the new America, the American government attempted to promote multiculturalism as the default identity of the society. From Ellis Island, all of the new immigrants were entrusted into the cacophony of cultures of the Lower East Side of Manhattan. By the thousands per day, they were dumped there, and each one of them was expected to survive. The materialistic concerns were of the prime importance; all else came to a halt. As a result, many cultures were lost, and in turn, new ones were born, albeit with a lack of any G-d except the vanilla G-d of the "Me" society. That G-d didn't come in any flavor, just a feel-good one, as per order. There were no other requests and no other needs. What was wrong with that picture?

The simplest and the most obvious one was the "Me society" which basically meant that each person must concentrate on whatever 'I' need and whatever can make "Me" feel numb from the pain and desolation. What separates a human from a "human animal" is the simplest desire to give without expecting any reciprocation. A child, by nature, is very kind and loving and often wants to share. As most of the youngsters of the immigrant society wanted to break away from the ways of their old-world society by assimilating and becoming Americanized, they decided to surrender their "ghetto mentality." They lived free of any societal limitations and became the Darwinian examples of "survival of the fittest." However, those who are so numb to inner pain and who are busy drowning out the inner voice can no longer know what love is or what a real relation-ship can be. Darwinism does not predicate these concepts to the human species because the main perspective of the "Me society" is "Me;" there is not even a possibility of anything else to develop. Love is simply translated as "Whatever suits 'My' needs" and 'Whatever makes 'me' happy - NOW." It is the perspective of an immature, self-centered adult caught in the human games of domination. The rest of the world is there to serve "my" needs. The instant gratification of fast cars, glamour and any sharp feeling of success are invigorating. No longer is there a need to belong to one's roots or a need for the love of giving. Those are left for the *losers* and the *"square"* ones.

The usual indication of a spoiled child is the adult who is still a "child at heart," who was never really trained to grow up. When this pseudo-adult turns thirty, he/she still lacks those necessary skills to be able to create a relationship with the opposite sex or anyone else. There is a constant desire to take, and never a demonstration of the vital components necessary to build a marriage relationship – being giving or having the strength to compromise. Because such individuals are selfish, and abusive, they might be drawn to like-minded partners... and the beautiful good qualities of interaction become absent. Only like-minded individuals will be drawn together because they really can't attract anyone else, being selfish, abusive, and non-compromising. In the end result, those beautiful and everlasting qualities are capable of remaining from generation to generation. Other qualities that are the color *gray*, at best, in the scheme of things, or just ugly, don't survive the ultimate test of time.

The "Me" society that has shed its yoke of caring has clearly failed, and the need for a better alternative to it should be more obvious today than ever before.

PART FOUR

SCIENTIFIC PERSPECTIVE

IN THE PAST, SCIENTISTS believed that the laws of determinism dictated that if all of the directives that govern all of the molecules and matter would be known, we would be able to predict the next stage and results. It's like a pool game: one shoots a white ball at a certain angle and the rest of the balls are predetermined by the velocity and trajectory. However, these days scientists propose that this theory has become a great deal more complicated because of the dynamics of the chaos theory and some others, like the butterfly[23] effect, and so, they remain as mysterious as ever. Scientists claim that the migrating pattern of butterflies from China to Hawaii or California could be one of the causes of typhoons since the force of billions of butterflies roving and clapping their wings are the cause of the severity of the weather patterns. In a similar vein, they say that if the rains are abundant or there is too much of the cold winter in China, the larvae of those butterflies would die and as a result, the power of the Typhoon would subside. Despite it all, those forces are extremely unpredictable, part of the aforementioned 'chaos theory', that throws scientific determinism out the proverbial window.

To make things even more complicated, those scientists use the concept of singularity and that of the "Big Bang" theory, the latest consensus of the "scientific perspective." They now begin to admit that perhaps there was a point of zero when time and space did not exist and when matter began to expand after being condensed to the size of a grain, becoming the universe, as we know it today. The scientists also theorize that perhaps there are even more dimensions than we can perceive and measure, and perhaps those dimensions are curled up unto themselves[24] in such a manner that our perspective cannot notice them. This can be compared to seeing a ship at a distance; one can only notice a tiny spec on the horizon. Although the ship is in reality extremely large and definitely there, it is almost deemed invisible. To a religious person, the concept of G-d, who is in charge of every aspect of our lives, is a comforting notion. That same concept to an unbeliever is quite frightening. Following the same logic as above, there may be other creations, like angels, that are not bound by time. To these creations, time might not be of consequence, and they may perceive us as being mere specs with our past and future as composites, merely inflating or deflating. The deductive reasoning is not an axiom and proverbial truth which scientists avow allegiance to. Dogmatism placed Copernicus on fire as much as theories of yesteryear have beens. Only maturity will allow the scientific community to acknowledge their fallacies and to grow. Religious perspective on the universe and beyond could be challenging to some but the possibilities are indeed mind-boggling.

COSMOLOGY

THE BIG BANG THEORY

ALTHOUGH THERE ARE THOSE scientists that propose that time is eternal and has no beginning and no end, and there are those that say that time was created after 'the big bang', the scientific theory of how the world came into being, attributing it to all the laws that govern physical reality and are described in cosmology, there are other views on the matter.

Another scientific school of thought claims that the reality of the universe as we see it, might be very different. In a more dimensional universe, 'the big bang' and subsequent expansion can be compared to a sort of soapsuds: beginning as nil, the more air it contains, the bigger and bigger it becomes. Time, as an independent axis of measurement, was, according to this group of scientists who espouse cosmology, expending extremely fast, but in real time only a few seconds was actually ticking away. The space of time planes might not have any connection whatsoever. Compared to a theory that scientists of only 40 years ago held dear to their heart, the Aristotelian Postulate, time is only a measurement of two bodies in motion. However that theory has been proven wrong upon the first astronaut arriving up in space and returning, losing almost a minute and a half.

In 1968, two Bell Labs scientists[25] stumbled upon further evidence to 'the big bang' theory. These scientists discovered an edge to our universe which still emitted radiation. Incidentally, one of the discoverers later on became an observant Jew. According to the expansionary universe perspective[26], those who propose the M-Brain Theory propose that the universe contains 80% dark space, which is not really observable. They can also explain why the pictures from the Hubble telescope seem to produce billions of galaxies in the making. They theorize that what a telescope is picking up is really an early stage of the universe when galaxies were being formed out of smaller clusters of stars and when some stars began imploding, creating black holes, or simply converting mass back into energy. They view our physical universe as a shard of billions of pieces[27] of shattered glass, so to speak. They theorize about an inflationary universe that could be created in 7 days of creation. It took scientists centuries to come to this conclusion, yet very ancient Jewish books spoke about it for millennia[2]! The scientists should be asking themselves why G-d decided it necessary to state that His intelligent design took six days, rather than one instant!

---

2   Eitz haim, Haim Vital

ARCHAEOLOGY AND TIME

E VER SINCE HAMMURABI'S CODEX, many other purported legends or truthful depictions or exaggerations of the era have existed. Numerous historians of different eras have unearthed them. Josephus, for example, was recording events for Romans, some of which seemed to contradict Jewish history, as is the case of the Maccabeeans. He also contradicted Christian history (since Josephus relegated Jesus to a mostly unknown sect/cult of Dead Sea 'Essenes").

In most histories of localized nations, they extol their proud moments while completely dropping out from history their losses and sometimes retroactively deleting the losing dynasties' names from the annals of their hieroglyphs. Historians of today are very prone to do the same thing when it comes to dealing with the Bible. They find many different ways to relegate biblical facts to 'made up stories', folklore and religious rhetoric rather than another authentically accurate historic portrayal of an age.

Archeologists of the past 300 years, usually because of sheer ignorance or intolerance to Religion, ignore the actual text in favor of their own bias. Amongst these types of scholars there are many kinds of theories regarding the existence of Abraham, the forefather of Semitic tribes. There many different opinions on the Abraham narrative. Some claim that it is a made up personality based on Hammurabi and his wars which was redacted 500 to 600 years later by King Hezekiah or his grandson. Others have 'even better ideas' that it was a fictitious personality to reconcile different ideological difficulties that later generations had come to. Even though there were documents found bearing 'Abram' or 'Ibrahim' as old as 3,600 years.[15]

| ta | ša | sû | w | ye | h | ûa | [w] |

"Shasu of Yahweh" inscription from the Temple of Amun, Sudan

Biblical critics and archeologists alike from the beginning of this century claimed that camels were not domesticated till at least 500 years after Abraham and the author didn't take that into account. But 50 years later historians discovered more and more clay cuneiform tablets which suggest that camels were imported from Mongolia in Arabia at least 4,000 years ago and were introduced to north Africa much later. But in the Assyrian empire camels and seals with depictions of camels[16] were around for at least 50 years before Abraham's birth. All those critics have long been disproven and gone down in history as being prejudiced at best or plain ignorant. Some had mistranslated urigitic texts claiming that some deity was busy eating their enemies yet in the end they were proven wrong and all of their postulations turned out to be based on a misreading of the word 'ana' with 'anat'. They wanted to see that letter at the end of that word on the tablet in order to write pure gibberish for 40 years. But, it turns out that this was just archaeological ignorance[17].

There are many examples dealing with Joseph. Take for example the price of a slave. Joseph is sold for twenty pieces of silver[18]. Slaves were cheaper beforehand, and they got increasingly more and more expensive later. Imagine someone five hundred years later putting in that detail. How would he know what the price of slaves were five hundred years earlier? He certainly wouldn't get it right by accident.

The investiture of Joseph as viceroy in Egypt follows the pattern from that period. He stood before Pharaoh and had to be shaved because the Pharaohs in that period were shaved. He had a collar put around his neck and a ring put on his finger. There are hieroglyphs of that specific procedure, and of riding in a chariot second to the king. The chariots were brought into Egypt with the Hyksos, a warring nation from Mesopotamia that conquered Egypt just at the perfect time and the only ones that would be fluent in a Semitic language like Aramaic. All of these details are accurate.

Kathleen Kenyon excavated Jericho during the 1950s. Most historians approximate Israelites/Hebrews [19]entry into the Promised Land with Joshua roughly[20] 1400 B.C.E. Mrs. Kenyon's acclaimed fame was to prove that the Joshua narrative didn't exist because he had to come to the region in 1400 B.C.E. , and her theory identified the collapse of the walls 150 years earlier. The story is told in the Book of Joshua, which describes Jewish warriors led by Joshua for six days. Marching his troops around the city, blowing rams' horns as per G-d's command. On the seventh day, the tumult of their shouting and the rams' horns caused the wall to collapse.

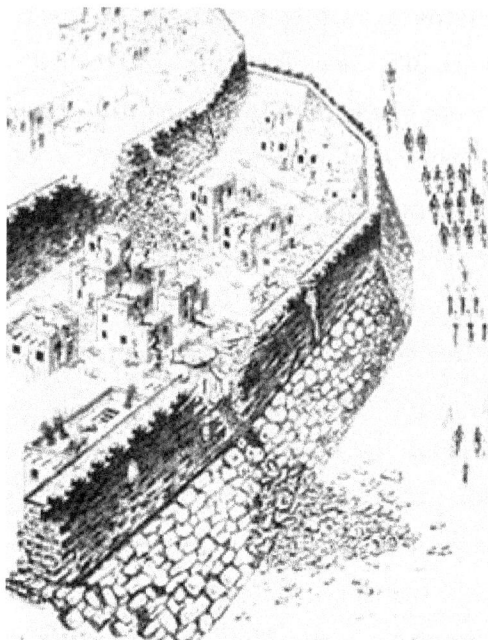

The event occurred after spring harvest[21] and the Israelites burned the city. The city did not fall as a result of a starvation siege, as was so common in ancient times, instead, Jericho was destroyed after seven days.

She based her arguments on the absence of imported Cypriot pottery that was imported into the area from 1550 to 1400 B.C.E., and she found none of it at Jericho. Therefore she concluded that Jericho must have been destroyed earlier than 1550 B.C.E. For this she was knighted. She says that there is a hundred and fifty year gap between the destruction of Jericho and the entry of the Jewish people into the land. In her historic perception the Jewish nation just attributed the story of Jericho being burned and fallen to their ancestors in order to glorify them.

But her conclusions were weak even at the time she published her findings and there were other historians[3] who argued against her conclusions based on several factors. She herself says that Jericho was not on any of the major trade routes and her conclusions were based upon two shafts into what she herself describes as the poor section of the city. Is that where you would expect to find imported pottery? She had been looking for the wrong kind of pottery, and in the wrong places. Her limited digging had occurred in what was a poor quarter of the city. This could account for her failure to find the expensive, imported Cypriot ceramics prevalent among many Canaanites

And then there is the region's seismic history. Jericho is in a rift valley, an unstable terrain prone to earthquakes. Many times in recorded history, geophysicists[22] say, earthquakes caused landslides and other disruptions leading to a blockage of the Jordan River for one or two days.

---

3. In the 1930s, another British archeologist, John Garstang, proposed a date of 1400 B.VC. for the destruction on the basis of an abundance of the simpler, everyday clay pots and bowls of that period pottery. But with Ms. Kenyon's reputation for more scientific field methods, Mr. Garstang's conclusions were largely ignored

"Israel is laid waste; its seed is not."

"Israel functioned as an agriculturally based or sedentary socioethnic entity in the late 13th century BCE one that is significant enough to be included in the military campaign against political powers in Canaan. While the Merneptah stela does not give any indication of the actual social structure of the people of Israel, it does indicate that Israel was a significant socioethnic entity that needed to be reckoned with."

ysrîr	fk.t	bn	pr.t	=f
Israel	waste	[negative]	seed/grain	his/its

Later on in the book of Joshua where the narrative describes the battle of Gibeon, it says that the sun had stood still, and that when this happened the Israelites attained another major victory. Israel did this by continuing to fight when the sun stood still, wearing out their enemies. Because scholars have been unable to explain the phenomenon, it has been disbelieved.

However, at about that same time, circa 1400 B.C., according to Aztec lore in Mexico, the sun failed to rise for a whole day in the City of the Gods, Teotihuacan (north of Mexico City). Likewise, it failed to rise for 20 hours in the Andes, according to Inca legends.

Since a day that does not end and a night that does not end are the same phenomenon in opposite parts of the world, the dating of the Israelite conquest at 1400 B.C., now corroborated by archeology at Jericho, would also confirm the tale of the sun's standing still in Gibeon.

DARWINIAN TIME

AFTER DARWIN LEFT THE Galapagos Islands he formulated what is until today held by most scientists and many lay people as the holy grail of perception of the world around us. All others who have any kind of religious semblance of mind either doubt the theory or simply call it irrelevant. With his ingenious masterstroke Darwin had colored the common understanding of all of life around us. He claimed some of the basic postulates of what is now known as social Darwinism - survival of the fittest. Utilizing this postulate he claimed that all of life as we know it, starting from simple cell structured amebas to humans, has always followed a natural selection of sorts which caused adaptation to the elements and the rise of more mature species. Ever so slightly changing their abilities to cope with the elements that they had to contend with, most began to branch and morph into different species of animals, may it be horse to giraffe to rhino and so on. Similarly, he claimed that the homosapien species had begun its development from ape like creatures down to modern-day man.

There were plenty of missing links in his chains of evolvement that he attributed to different members of the animal kingdom. For example he claimed that Neanderthal was a missing link between humans as we know it and the ape species.

But for the past three thousand years there have been none found. As archeologists continue to dig and postulate they still cannot resolve most of these mysteries of our existence. They made the discovery of "Lucy," a 3-foot tall female chimpanzee that was dated to roughly three million years old. Yet this creature had one abnormality: its hind legs had enough muscle tone to identify it as walking upright. Any later remains that scientists found did indicate more and more similarity to humans except one thing, the bone and muscle texture around the tongue[37], which indicate communication skills rather than grunts. This was absent until remains of 15,000 years old, which seem to have a more demonstrative ability to talk. Yet the remains of Neanderthal still were found until 10,000 ago and then abruptly disappearing without any explanation. How could these primate humanoids have vanished without a trace while living in parallel with our ancestors, one group never mingling with the other?

The small-scale domestication and some minimal agrarian practices were found around the ancient Canaanite society of roughly 10,000 years ago, yet they did not indicate a major village of even a hundred people. The burial practices that archaeologists and paleontologists attribute to humans as we know them do exist but some seemed haphazard without a mound or a family plot, more like bodies simply put in shrouds and buried. Recently in the middle of the Sahara, scientists have found nomadic people who would herd cattle on small-scale. The average height of this populous was definitely over six feet tall, which is extremely unlike the local populous whose remains were found at the same site dating to roughly five thousand years ago.

The actual city-states and full-blown agrarian practices and trade of domesticated cattle was only found around modern-day Iraq around the city state of "UR" at the same Biblical location of the "UR KASDIM" or Chaldean, as known in scientific circles. These date back no earlier than five thousand years ago. Yet anything found predating that did not demonstrate the same sophistication of wall building or burial or farming and domestication practices. Actual cities with markets and organized societies were not found anywhere earlier than the latter part of 3,000 BCE.

The scientific community has recently tried to tie all of their findings to the discoveries of large meteorite the size of Rhode Island that created the Gulf of Mexico, thus making two continents. Another meteorite, they claimed, shifted the Earth's axis and so on. In their postulations it seems that these cataclysmic events took out all of the living creatures and their food for at least a hundred years because the smoke and ash that came about would not clear up for that length of time. Further, they suggest that there might have been six or so events like that, which spurred major climate change and total annihilation of any preexisting flora and fauna.

Actually, all of today's oil supplies come from that age. Many scientists have now come to a consensus that the development of all known species on earth didn't follow a gradual selection as Darwin predicted, but rather made major jumps that can't be accounted by any means. And as mentioned before, to the great surprise and chagrin of the scientific community we have learned that Neanderthal and Mankind of the early Bronze Age have very little in common except the gene pool, and the two species lived side by side never interfering with one another.

What is even more puzzling is that some of the cosmologists used to claim that the Big Bang came about as a totally random event, which is completely absurd. As Dr. Lanza has personally admitted, "If there were one-billionth of a difference in the mass of the Big Bang, you couldn't have galaxies. If the gravitational constant were ever-so-slightly different, you couldn't have stars, including the sun, and you would just have hydrogen. There are 200 parameters like this. We now have people out there talking about an intelligent design, saying 'God' is the explanation. But it is really because quantum theory is right." That is what, at least for some scientists intent on denying the existence of God, passes for "logic."

JEWISH PERSPECTIVE ON TIME

The foremost principle one has to understand is the most basic tenant of Jewish belief of monotheism: that G-d is indivisible, beyond time or any kind of physical existence - without any beginning or end, without any purpose that the human mind can attribute to Him[4]. Furthermore, the Talmud tells us that it is inappropriate to discuss the act of creation with more than two[5] because one has to be familiar with the audience and understand their line of thinking. Should a wrong conclusion be drawn from the discussion of the deep secrets of creation, the one who delivered the discourse will be held accountable. If those two get disciples and disseminate the false ideas to the masses, the initial Sage will be held responsible.

Throughout the millennia, our sages always used euphemisms to discuss the details of creation when speaking or writing to a forum that was directed to more than two recipients. They followed the equation that revealing one detail would cover up twice as much[6]. But the verse "the honor

---

4. 13 principles,Rambam
5. Talmud hagiga 13 a
6. Talmud nidorim 20,b

of the King's daughter is to uncover the hidden[7]", refers to seeking and understanding the hidden in order to show the glory of G-d. It thus encourages the revelation or shedding of light on one of the greatest mysteries: the creation. Notwithstanding this verse, if one takes the simplistic approach that the mighty Hashem created the universe in a fully developed form, all that is presently at hand could have been created as such. The counter argument then disputes the point in time when the universe could have been created; it follows that along that line of thinking, the universe, indeed, could have been created only five minutes ago, making the initially presented case moot.

The first verse in the Bible proclaims that "In the beginning, G-d created Heaven and Earth.[8]" Does this indicate some sort of time process? Furthermore, the sun and the moon and all other celestial bodies began to function or emit light on the fourth day in a sense that relates to human observation. One of the Haggadic sages asked why the Torah stated "and it was evening and it was morning, the first day." He expounds on the question by saying that since the verb 'was' is written in the past tense and not in the present, The Torah is telling us that the evening (time) was present previously and that, in actuality, there were other evenings and other creations that G-d found to be unproductive; consequently, He destroyed them[9].

---

7. Psalms 40,14
8. Genesis 1,1
9. Medrash Raba 2,3

The Bible explains that the Creator's process of the creation of the known universe took six days and that He rested on the seventh day. Does that mean that the universe became fully functioning at that time? Complicating matters further, we know that the world cannot exist more than seven thousand years[10]. We also know that G-d destroyed certain creations prior to the onset of the function of the universe. Based upon those details, our sages concluded that there must be seven such periods of seven thousand years for G-d's universe to continue. Does the figure of 49,000 years translate somehow into human years? One sage explained the phenomenon through the Book of Psalms (90,4) where the passing of one day was like a thousand years to

---

10. Talmud hagiga, 13 b.

KOSHER TIME

human accounting. In this vein, a year would be equal to 365,250 years[28] to us. By multiplying the 49,000 years that G-d apparently will allow the known universe to exist before disintegrating it, we come to an equivalent of 17,897,250,000 years of human comprehension. All this, however, does not correlate to our own concept of time; i.e., twenty four hours and so on.

If one simply pays attention to the Bible narrative from a certain point, the reader will see that all of the chronology seems to dictate logic. For example, the city built by Cain himself was named after the birth of his son Enoch in the year 622 from creation or 3138 B.C.E. The Bible also attributes the art of forging metal by developing a method of casting melted bronze and gold into cooking tools and armor to Tubal Cain, the son of Lamech, who was born in 777 or 2985 B.C.E. All of these dates seem to correlate with the archeologist's idea of when the first city-states were developed and when the Bronze Age began. Despite the apparent facts, however, scientists disregard this information and relegate it to old wive's tales.

There are other scientists of Jewish lineage who enjoy connecting certain verses to events in cosmology and other inconsistencies between the Bible and the prevailing scientific opinion, attempting to make cohesion. Yet different scientific ideas emerge and prevail over the course of time, and so these Jewish scientists make their opinions obsolete. They point out, for example, that the Neanderthal Man had as much cranial capacity as now yet for a hundred thousand years did not make use of it and had disappeared as mysteriously roughly

14,000 ago. Then, ten thousand years ago, the simplistic farming skills and small settlements were formed because of the cranial capacity that evolved through the "natural selection" of the elements. Afterwards, roughly five thousand years ago, actual cities and states began to form and the human species essentially learned from their own mistakes and made advances upon others' ingenuity. Indeed, it is possible to make a connection from current scientific discussions and suppositions to the actual words of the Torah, yet pinning those same scientific speculations to the holy word is ludicrous.

At this point, I would like to divert the discussion to others who suggest that the verse "and G-d's spirit hovered on top of the abyss," indicates that the primordial universe is some sort of black hole and G-d's spirit is in the middle of it all, expanding space. But this seems a little bit too incredible. As our sages point out, the actual spiritual constriction/*zimzum*[29], and the burst of rays of light going to the center and annihilating the center, happened more than once. Doing so, the Almighty left those obliterated pieces of raw energy and space alone and made a new constriction of his 'unbound energy', allowing for empty space in which He could shape the universe once again, this time with less energy.

Even though the idea of the 'big bang' evolved only in the past 50 years because of Einstein[30]'s theory of relativity, he claimed that matter and raw energy, like sun rays or electricity, are the same, and interchangeable[31], based upon a mathematical equation. His theory explains that mass, if thrown at twice the speed of light (a constant), will become energy and therefore relevant to its source. In the layman's terminology this means that water and vapor in the clouds are the same product, yet in a different consistency. Einstein also proposed that the Universe, at its initial state, did not follow the laws of quantum mechanics or any law that we can comprehend at the present stage except through the label of super density or 'singularity'. Then Professor Stephen Hawking, who is an avid atheist, proposed the idea of singularity, an expansionist universe and M/P- Brain Theories, and claimed the possibility of a Creator plausible. As of five years ago, there is another branch of mathematicians, headed by Professor Brian Greene[32] at Columbia University. This branch proposes that the universe is actually a giant shard of space (a broken glass jar, where each and every broken piece of tiny glass is connected to the next in a string fashion). It claims that all known matter is made of the same particle, which has 26 dimensions[33]. Some of these dimensions are curved unto themselves and are too small for us to detect.

It is true that one can base certain rabbinical arguments upon the actual current arguments amongst the scientific community whose ideas are largely proven and disproven almost regularly. Our Rabbis disagree about what exactly was the living spirit that Hashem had breathed into the first man. Was it the power to be able to communicate intricate abstract ideas verbally? Or was it the living spirit (an extra layer of the spiritual soul that allowed the first man to be able to cleave to the living spirit of G-d) that enabled man to become more like an angel, yet with the capacity to discern the potential future with reality and an actual power of choice? Or was it, as the Rabbis call *"odom sihly"* – comprehending man?

The Rabbis do believe in anthropology, as seen in the example of Hillel, himself, when he stated that certain people have long flat feet because they walk a great deal on the sand and that others have flatter facial features based upon their environment. Hillel's observations indicated that a people's surroundings shape their features with the passage of time. Another rabbi gave an analogy based on the manner in which running water can break through a rock. If a soft element of water can erode a hard rock, then the gentle words of our Torah can turn a person into a great sage of enormous capacity who can influence others and shape the future. With these basic perspectives of anthropology, one can draw certain conclusions and, at the same time, state that there is a distinction between the Neanderthal and the Original Man, taking Torah where it was never meant to be.

The Rabbis draw a distinction between the act of Creation (ex nihilo): between forming and making, and what was before Creation and of everything known. One of the basic books of esoteric thought describes in detail "the Big Bang," explaining how G-d, whose entity is totally spiritual in nature, is capable of creating lower levels of spirituality or conduits to the physical world. The Rabbis explain it the same way, as the spiritual realm functions are in similitude with the physical world functions. Because of this, the "Big Bang" was described in detail, down to the immeasurable ray of light burning substance - the size of a grain exploding and making our known space.

The first verse "In the beginning of *'He created'*, **G-d** of the heavens and of the 'earth'," reversing the order of G-d and created, might sound grammatically wrong and superfluous, as all of the commentaries point out. The Septuagint (the seventy Jewish scholars whom King Tholomei had placed to translate the Bible) rendered it as "G-d created," since in Hebrew, "ברא" is translated as "He created," diverting it from the literal translation. Our Sages were actually concealing a great mystery of the word G-d *"Elokim,"* whose numerical value "1+30+5+10+40," equaling 86, is the same as the word, nature, *'HaTeVaH'*, equaling "5+9+2+70." Literally, the word "Elokim" translates as a judge, rendering this aspect of G-d, a true judge – measure for measure. Some rabbis explain that this name reflects the natural laws of physics; i.e., for every action there is a counter action, or laws of conservation of energy. This depicts that "In the beginning" He created the nature (physical laws) of the Heaven (literally meaning fire and water) and of the Earth. Through this, we see that in order for G-d to create a physical entity, He needed to create physical laws, a glove of sorts, with which physicality could become conceived.

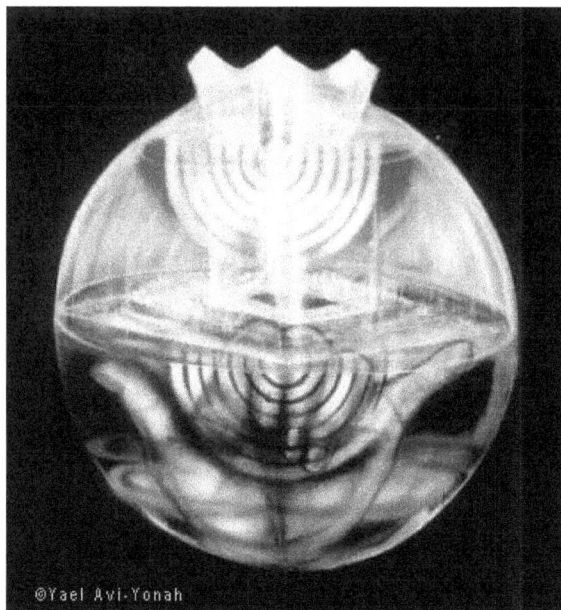

©Yael Avi-Yonah

For those who know biblical grammar, the extra articles of "את אה" "of the" are also superfluous. The grammatically definitive article, "the" – "ה," requires "of" – "את," but if the definitive article is not mentioned then the "את" is not necessary either. This leads us to an explanation that the phases of creating hydrogen dioxide (water) "מים" to the highest degree of heat – "אש," and the planetary space "הארץ," occurred from the first till the 22d stages. Interestingly, the article "את" is made up of the first and the last letters of the Jewish alphabet numerically being one and twenty two.

The verse, 'These are generations of Heaven and Earth' that are written at the conclusion of the sixth day, presents a major dichotomy. Were the creations following the sequences as they were pronounced or were they following some other order? The explanation is resolved with an allegory: the olive tree branches produced olives which were ripe and some others which were not yet ripe; as each day of creation came about different olives became ripe for picking. The initial ability to produce those olives, however, was made possible at the point of implantation and when the roots took hold. Hashem created all of his creations initially with His initial act of creation. Then as His Creation began to unfold at each consecutive turning point He would began a new chapter of His creation. With it all of the details of that specific creation began to formulate and take place.

A deeper analysis of the first word "In the Beginning," "בראשית," reveals something odd, in the sense that the term is not used that many times. Literally, one cannot really say that it means "In the beginning of," but rather, in the middle of the beginning. The Hebrew term for what initially was being created would more accurately be: "בראשונה ברא" and not "ברא בראשית" Now, what preceded the creation of the world might be a moot question to some because what does it matter if there was no space or any kind of dimensionality. The Medrash[26], however, clearly proclaims that the Torah – the Bible – was created two thousand years before the actual creation of the world and that G-d had to wait for a thousand generations[27] before He could give the Torah. Paradoxically, there were only 26 generations from Adam until Moses. Where could all of the other 974 generations have gone?

The two above statements regarding G-d's creation and the differing unsatisfactory universes created prior to ours are extremely difficult to understand. Were these different generations of people or were they generations made up of other types of rational creations that were physical in nature or spiritual? Were they similar to Adam before coming to the physical reality of the world and leaving the spirituality or abstractness of the "Garden of Eden?" Were they just like Adam, living elongated lives[11] and never having to succumb to the elements or any other ailments, and perhaps never even perishing?

The Talmud explains that there are 12 constellations, each having 30 "army's" (perhaps galaxies), each containing 30 legions(Quadrants) and each containing 30 captains(sectors). In each, there are 30 sergeants who are in charge of 365,000 stars, cumulatively becoming a luminary of 14 trillion stars[5]. This calculation happens to be the rough approximation based upon the density and distance to the edge of the universe made by today's scientists! An outsider should thus ask himself: "What in the world were those Rabbis of roughly 2,400 years ago, with their long white beards, doing approximating the amount of stars in the universe? Additionally, where did such a large calculated number come from; and how did they make such an assumption merely based upon the amount of verses in psalms that are located here and there?" In another place the Rabbis discuss the comets that crashed into the earth, killing all of the animals and shifting the axis of the globe and the

---

11. Rabeinu BeHai explains that these generations lived in an era that had little to do with our concept of time. He explains that each of these generations either lived only 2 years and not 35 of ours, or perhaps their 2 years where like a thousand of ours.

weather and covering the planet with water. Perhaps scientists should once again look into the Bible now as grown ups and admit that there are things that even they can learn from it.

In the end, there can be no contradiction between true science and true religion. Both attempt to comprehend the reality of this universe we live in. Mutual respect and cooperation between the scientific disciplines and the sages of religion could yield unimaginable benefits of knowledge and insight for all of humanity.

PART FIVE

BEAUTY

EVERYONE HAS THEIR OWN personal opinion on beauty. Some see the surreal beauty of things, their true value and their ultimate destiny, while others look at the superficial type. Vincent van Gogh saw the beauty of a sunflower plant. He painted it in such surreal colors, thereby making certain aspects stand out, while diminishing others, and bringing out entire new facets of beauty that could not be discerned before. However, there is a great deal of unseen and unnoticed beauty that G-d has designed. The most obvious elements pertaining to this are the northern lights, water that falls at a rate of a million gallons per second, or nature itself. Botanists see beauty in a plant's cells that multiply for no apparent reason. The botanists can explain why cells multiply and how chlorophyll turns sunlight into a source of energy and be amazed by the design. Some might even see the most profound beauty in the electron, the proton or in many other simple elements which make up the world around us. Some beauty is eternal, withstanding the test of time, while other aspects of beauty last only as long as the lifespan of a butterfly, fluttering in the sun and displaying its beauty to the world.

The structure of the makeup of our universe and the matter around us follows a specific order that has laws, like gravity, electricity and many others. Some scientists see beauty in how

G-d has manipulated nature, causing the simple bonding of some electrons, spinning around protons that turn into the grand picture of the universe we see every day. It was only during the modern-day era of science that scientists were able to deduce or discover the true nature of the universe, and to explain some of the forces that hold it together. Sometimes, with pure luck, by proving or disproving other's theories about the atomic structure or the force behind each atom they came to their revelations. At precisely the peak point of these proofs of the multi dimensionality of the space around us, the scientists understood that they had barely scratched the surface of the pure and limitless explanation to G-d's façade called the universe.

Imagine a solar system just like ours, where there are planets revolving around the sun. On each orbiting ring there are planets except in this system where there are two planets on the first orbit, then on the next orbit there are four planets and on the next there are eight and so on. Since the circumference of the orbit gets longer with every consecutive orbit there are spaces left for more and more planets and because of the laws of gravity, these planets follow the very exact path, yet do not collide into their neighboring rings and do not fall into the sun. This was the picture that Professor Mendeleev saw when he designed his table of all known molecules, leaving blanks where he intuitively knew that there should be a basic substance consisting of a molecule which should have that amount of planets or electrons.

Professor Mendeleev established that a molecule that does

not have a full ring of perfect multiples (i.e. the last orbit only has five electrons and not eight and has a negative charge of three because it is always looking for some electrons to fill in the chain) would be more predisposed to join into another molecule to construct an entire new bond where they would share some of these planets: the many electrons that go around beyond the sun, and the protons, in union with the neutrons – both making up the core of the sun's gravitational or electromagnetic pull. This beautiful picture gave birth to modern-day plastics and chemistry. Today we are very content to use the synthetics that the previous century's Professor Mendeleev thought was a possibility and now are a reality. The great production of synthetics came to being because of those that were able to discern that perfect beauty of G-d's creation, and utilized His design to construct and improve, thereby allowing mankind to live better and more economically. That is the beauty that G-d seeks to embark unto mankind.

Professor Fox[36] was able to create an organic substance out of inorganic components. He created simple amino acids, the basic building block of a living cell, with the use of carbon dioxide, methane, ammonia and water vapor, together with spark discharges. He attempted to demonstrate that with the random use of electricity, a basic substance of living matter could be created. But in reality, he barely began to uncover how much wisdom and beauty our Creator has implanted in His creation.

What he actually was able to demonstrate that any atom is very predisposed to become some sort of substance, whether organic or inorganic in nature. Molecules can be combined into forming polymers, plastics, or any other matter. Today's doctors are making body parts out of simple skin tissue. They have learned how to convert simple living cells with the use of certain viruses into stem cells, and doing so they reverse the process that creates each one of us.

When a famous great rabbi[12] saw a budding flower, he did not simply pass by and perceive it to be just another aspect of nature. Rather, he saw the Power that sustains it, that makes it blossom and come alive, seeing beyond time. He was so in awe of the flower and with it, G-d's true Hand that it took his breath away and he desired to become closer to G-d – the Original Source of all living things. He considered the miracle of life of the flower to be as great as the actual splitting of the Red Sea. In that same aspect, time is not just something we have to live with, but it is a creation designed specifically for us and given to us as a gift. Time is a form of energizing electricity. It is an opportunity to fill ourselves with life.

There are definitely some examples of how scientists took the beauty of creation and reverted it to a destructive force of unimaginable magnitude, like using mustard gas on civilians or dropping nuclear weapons on populated cities, and obliterating all living things. The use of the electron became only imaginable in the beginning of this century. Professor Einstein and others theorized that if one takes one electron and forces it unto another there would be an immense explosion, that of the magnitude similar to that on the surface of the sun. They

12 R. Kareliz, The Chazon Ish

knew that due to the immensity of the sun, its gravity would cause all the surface matter which is in a perpetual state of gas form. However, at the surface, where substance begins to become extremely condensed, a nuclear reaction is a reoccurring process. This process causes a chain reaction of many other more powerful explosions to take place, which forces the cycle to continue indefinitely, some of these more extreme explosions emitting plasma initially consisting of helium and hydrogen gasses. Once they break the gravitational pull they become radiation of immense magnitude which produces solar winds. In the same manner, they proposed that, just as helium and hydrogen gas that is present in the extreme temperatures of 100,000 degrees, causes electrons in extreme motion to fall into each other's path and constantly erupt into nuclear explosions, a simulation could be created in a lab.

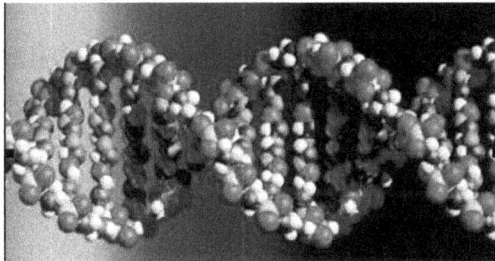

One of the scientists had detected that when uranium is exposed to the sun or unearthed from its dormant state, its decay into simpler substances, like radon, hydrogen and many other gases begins. They even proposed and attempted early experimentation of creating a nuclear power station. They tried to place a couple of rods, made up of some uranium, into water and observe the results. As they predicted, the water started to boil and heat up to immense temperatures. They tried to calculate how much of those basic elements would be required in order to cause a controlled explosion – one which they could fore-determine and thus be able to shield themselves just adequately enough prior to its onset to safely be capable to deduce the unimaginative amount of energy released afterwards.

We all know what erupted out of the Manhattan project and what course history has taken afterwards, but it definitely became a deterrent for some nations, making certain that each one would not pulverize the other a hundred times over.

But with every good there always is born the possibility for bad. When Albert Einstein wrote a letter to President Roosevelt urging him to take his research seriously, Hitler, who was on the rise to power at the time, was planning to do the same. Truman accepted Einstein's offer, provided him with a professorial job, and a prominent place in the Manhattan project. The Manhattan project was responsible for producing the first nuclear weapon. However, Einstein until his last day was very distraught over his invention that had so much potential, yet brought with it a possible Armageddon.

We, too, could benefit from such a cautious approach. The great beauty of all that surrounds us should be seen as the Creator's gift, to be appreciated by us and nurtured, as well as protected from the destruction that the human mind too often conceives of as a perverse replacement for genuine beauty.

THEOLOGY OF BEAUTY

S OME SEE BEAUTY IN the Bible itself: the symmetry between different ideas that reveal a very new and profound truth. In the beginning of the book of Genesis, G-d created "male and female" into one soul, and breathed it into a newly shaped body. He made it capable of thinking abstractly in order to be able to communicate with G-d, since the rudimentary level before this living soul, was able to communicate only to the animal kingdom. Then, as time progressed, G-d saw that, in this condition of uniqueness, man was not good and He said, "It is not good for him to be alone." G-d split the soul into two separate entities, male and female, making the female as a helpmate to Man "to assist in opposition." At the end of this creation, G-d exclaimed that from henceforth every male shall leave his parents' home and "cleave unto his wife" and create a profoundly new and different household.

Our sages find the following difficulty in understanding this verse: Why did G-d initially create the prototype of a mankind by fusing male and female into one body and then separating them in order that they should become as one in unison? The sages point out that the only way humankind will able to grow spiritually and become more saintly is by following G-d's original design. By entering into a marriage, and working on all the obstacles that present themselves in that union of man and woman - two uniquely different personalities, characteristics and entities – the possibility of all aspects of human growth presents itself. This is in total contrast to the original design of an angel, where the essential soul is not capable of any spiritual growth.

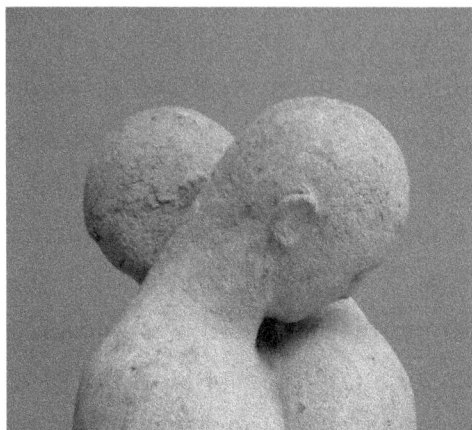

On a similar note, beauty cannot be understood as theoretical and ethereal or rather straightforward and obvious.

The obvious example personifying this paradox is the episode involving Judith, who initiated the Maccabean rebellion that ultimately caused Hellenization to stop and Israel to gain its independence. Judith boldly walked into the hall of her marriage ceremony without any clothes on, shocking all present, and giving grounds for a possible death sentence to be decreed upon her. What she was attempting to do, however, was to make a statement questioning the public's apathy to the Greek immoral practice of taking Jewish brides for the Greek governor prior to their marriage. She was boldly questioning their devotion to physical beauty which personified Hellenism. Hers was a statement of protest to this and all that the Greeks attempted to deny the Jewish people. Following her act, all of the Maccabean men reacted by taking up arms, thus beginning the revolt.

The Hebrew word for beauty, and Greek culture and Hellenism as a concept, is not consistently related. Beauty can only be appreciated and seen if it is in the right perspective and placed in its proper role. Ideals of beauty are deeply rooted in our common humanity. It has to do with the Creator's vision for the completeness of male and female.

PITFALLS OF HUMAN BEAUTY

THE SUPERFICIAL BEAUTY CAN also be seen in many different layers. Upon the birth of a first precious child, both parents devote a great deal of their energy and love to it, attempting to imbue it with the most they have to offer. They give of the warmth of their souls, and the light of their intellect, yet their child sometimes turns out not what they both had expected - a little bit selfish, a little bit sarcastic, and a great deal too witty for his/her own good. What happened, they ask themselves. Where did they go wrong? The answer sometimes is obvious, but very difficult to see with the naked undiscerning eye. The first child usually prepares his parents for the rest of the siblings, ascertaining that his parents are attuned to his/her every need and want. Initially, they take care of all his/her possible needs – after all, he/she is totally helpless and genuinely endearing. But the pampering never stops there. The child feels empowered by the attention that he/she received when he/she was very young and progressively wants and demands the same as was offered before, putting the loving parents in a bind. Can they possibly take care of every need and can they give into every want? Did they create a monster, and not a most beautiful and precious child. At this point, the true beauty or lack of it, begins to show. How does one give away those beautiful emotions to a child that was trained to be abusive and is not very cognizant of anyone else's needs or wants? The cycle had started, but there is always hope and perhaps the parents will realize that a selfish child is the most helpless creation they could have created. The person who has the fine character of sharing and is willing to compromise is the one who is truly beautiful and will be prepared to interact properly with others.

The usual sign of a once spoiled child is the adult who is still a child at heart and who was never really trained to grow up. This pseudo-turning-thirty-adult still lacks those necessary skills to be able to create a relationship with the opposite sex or anyone else. He/She always desires to take, and never even displays the desire to be giving or to give in – something that another party usually looks for in a potential match. The mind of such an immature individual, even if truly beautiful, does not have the proper tools to be able to bestow those wonderful gems stored within it to a potential partner or anyone else. Only like-minded individuals will be waiting for some sort of companionship from him or her because, by being selfish, abusive and non-compromising, they really cannot attract anyone else. In the end result, those beautiful and everlasting qualities are capable of remaining from generation to generation. Other qualities that, at best, are neutrally gray, or just plain ugly, do not survive the ultimate test of time. They are destined, quite appropriately, for annihilation.

PART SIX

TIME AS A CAUSER

TIME, ACCORDING TO OUR sages, is looked at as a spiral of sorts that is continuously attempting to force us to go upward, challenging us into making us better human beings. Once in a while, we may have a déjà-vu of sorts reminding us that we had done this or that misdeed before. That specific déjà-vu, be it a situation or confrontation or even a decision on our part, will repeat itself inadvertently over and over again, and perhaps tell us something. It might be a different situation or a different set of people or location than before, but the sense of being there at another point in time - that nagging feeling that this road was once taken and apparently not successfully traveled on - is present and tangible. G-d uses these situations of déjà- vu in order to help us grow and not stumble again, making time take on a completely different meaning. Unlike the deterministic view of science, King Solomon predicted in the Book of Ecclesiastes that this power of causality would take on new meaning.

The seasons play a major role, not only for the time of planting, reaping and winnowing, but also for the holidays that are associated with them. During the holiday of Sukkot, we commemorate the spectacular Exodus out of Egypt, as well as the glorious "Clouds Of Glory" that shielded us from the elements. But the essential fact – that of a whole people leaving the concrete shelters, be it houses, mansions or apartments, to rickety, unsteady booths, topped with miniscule roofs of wooden planks or bamboo - sets a tone of G-d running the show. For seven days we are reminded of our own fragility before G-d and, despite that, G-d in His infinite wisdom bestows His "Divine Will" upon us and provides us - according to our belief in Him, our utilization of His influence, the sanctity in which we conduct our lives, and the G-dliness that we allow to become a part of us - with favorable future prospects.

The cyclical nature of time is part of the very fabric of the universe. It permeates our lives and helps to shape our destiny. Our destinies are truly in our hands but the destiny of humanity still flows under the tutelage of the Divine plan.

DORMANT GIFTS

FROM ITS VERY FIRST breath, a newborn is extremely fragile, and needs constant attention. He requires continuous feedings, care and love. Yet he is endowed with many gifts of reasoning: that of judging, discerning and being able to deduce. Immediately following birth, a baby has certain automatic reactions. When in pain, a baby screams; when happy, a baby coos. Pediatricians might even present other "instinctual manners" that exhibit how a baby understands what needs to be accomplished yet does not have the maturity in ability to do. However, when the baby does gain the ability, the initial knowledge is lost. For example, an infant instinctually understands how to walk and crawl during the first couple of weeks in this world, but it has neither enough muscles nor the strength to sustain himself. By the time the baby gains an adequate amount of muscle mass to stand, however, the baby forgets what to do and must resort to the laborious experience of trial and error.

The internalization of facts, like who is "Mommy," how her voice sounds, when is the time to play or nap, and who has soft hands, goes through a thorough analysis. The brain begins to develop and grow. These gifts will not make themselves apparent, yet the processing and internalization of these minuscule facts goes on constantly. Despite initially being dictated by the constant hours of sleep induced by his needs, a child begins to learn that day is when one is active and night is when one sleeps. Then the child begins to notice what one does to get attention, where to find food, and most importantly, how to be cute. All these observations, however, will not be put into use until the child will learn how to communicate.

Initially, this involves an ordinary process of give and take – baby cries—"mommy" comes, baby stops – parents leave. This is a beginning to all of our human issues of control over our self-expressions – when we demand to be heard, sometimes we are totally unaware of others' needs, and we are selfish – childish. Adults who are demanding, never graduating from this stage of self-absorption, are detrimental to themselves, according to Freud or his followers. From this elementary stage, we train our personalities to be manipulative and controlling of others and use it to our advantage. An example of such a self-preservation type of motive is the initial screaming of a child that lets the caretaker know that his needs must be met. As time goes on, however, it evolves into a different sort of problem. Just as the physical body goes through a metamorphosis by maturing ever so slightly, similarly, the intellectual capability expands to allow an even greater level of understanding of the previously acquired concepts. The intellectual processes of an infant not only matures with age, initially thinking that the world begins and ends with "mommy and Teddy bear," but keeps developing well into advanced age, conceptualizing the greater parts of the world around, understanding greater details and abstractions of nature and its inner workings. However, the emotional and spiritual growth might not even ever begin, or might remain on a basic self-preservation level.

Human growth, in our capacities and our potential, is clearly intended to be a lifelong process. Physical growth is only the beginning, the precursor of far greater developments as the human mind and soul awaken to all of the realities of our wonderful existence.

INVENTIVENESS

IMAGINATION IS THE MOTHER of invention, as most would stipulate. Necessity is what spurred progress as the Industrial Revolution has proven. It propelled humankind into the twentieth century, moving the vast majority of the population from an agrarian economy to production lines and city dwelling. But along the with this unprecedented progress came evils like child labor, exploitation, single woman households, opium dens, etc. Every remedy that different societies provided came about two-fold, as the "cures" that were proposed often brought about their own problems. The imbalance amongst different sectors of societies between the wealthy and poor, educated and illiterate and gainfully employed and the moochers continued. Polarization amongst these groups increased and along came high crime rates, gangs and gangsters. Human imagination couldn't even fathom the evils that were born from this situation, such as genocides, concentration camps and human extermination simply based upon one's religion. Theologians were puzzled how human societies and human nature had spiraled out of control into an abyss that was worse than hell, if ever imagined. Could our imagination have brought this about? Did the likes of Mother Teresa begin to be outnumbered by the likes of Hitler and other dictators of the world? Humanness has dwindled amongst humanity down to the level of barbarism and cannibalism.

However, most do not realize that Imagination is the most sacred tool that G-d has endowed mankind with. In the biblical narrative the "angel" who resembled the snake began his discussion with Eve by purporting to be a very charming car salesman telling her that the Tree of Knowledge will allow her to create worlds and become an independent agent outside of the Creator's providence. It is true that with the knowledge of good came the desire that was not yet known and with the consumption of the snake's sales pitch, the evil became part of human nature becoming an antecedent to the goodness that was not yet realized in human emotion. This gave the opportunity of revealing further good through human amalgamation of G-d's reality with the use of the knowledge, which came about instantaneously once the fruit was consumed. This angel/Satan was able to induce Eve into consuming the fruit, through the use of guile and seduction, generating in her those emotions. With the consumption of the fruit of knowledge humankind had also begot freedom of choice seeing good and bad in everything and able to choose. Once filled with doubt, which previously had not been present in G-d's creation, Man became a partner in creation being able to procreate not only in the physical sense but in the metaphysical sense as well. This freedom of choice made mankind have the potential of being elevated above the angels yet if succumbing to the vice becoming a partner with the angel of death or the snake/master of destruction. The guile that the snake used is called "being naked/brazen" and also becomes the ability of mankind to be inventive. Being able to challenge the common wisdom of conformity, seeing the need for improvement, accomplishing it. Some say that that was the purpose of the entire creation, G-d planning and implanting the situation of the Tree of Knowledge. But they point out that the angel did too good of a job implementing the Creator's plan, forcing himself into the scheme of creation, not being apart and subservient to the grand design. For that G-d disavowed any connection to the angel of death, allowing him to rule over human mediocrity, never being able to come back to G-d and sing his praise and devotion; instead, he just became an accuser in front of throne of the Creator.

Man has an intuitiveness with which we are able to see the potential in everything, may it be planting a tree and seeing it produce fruit to being able to release the energy of an atom producing nuclear energy. This was the most crucial development that set us apart from the rest of creation, making us unique. Throughout the ages man has used this intuitiveness constructively, benefiting all of humanity, or destructively, annihilating the surrounding cultures and nations, bringing time to a standstill or worse reversing it. Throughout the millennia there were sellers of the future, for example Nimrod, who had built the tower which caused schism in humanity, giving birth to a multitude of nations, causing each to go its separate way, further settling the planet yet never again uniting for any reason. Or Napoleon, who had claimed to have a lofty goal of emancipating all from monarchy yet caused the republic to be ruled by a mob. In our modern day we have a whole industry dedicated to this lofty goal of selling their twisted perception of right and wrong, inculcating us with their salacious mindset – "Entertainment".

The authors of old were able to sell their brand of imagination through the use of imagery and verse which "enlightened" the masses. Yet settling the roots of their desires upon others, perverting and changing them. Today, movie studios and producers have taken over the sinister job of enlightenment, selling to the world ideas of being counterproductive, becoming onlookers, watching life, not experiencing it or being inventive. Most spend a third of their life being cuffed to the couch watching mindless nonsense and hence becoming brain dead. We have become connoisseurs of the masterful art of story telling from the art of paintings, theater, books or the screen. By screening other's imagery and their imagination, severing from the neck down, abdicating willingly decision making that would be based on logic and not on their brand of Yellow Journalism. But what happened to the inventiveness that had spurred the societal growth for millennia?

This imagery that others purport unto us from kindergarten gives us the ideology of being complicit and conforming, becoming conformists – Lazy[13]. The great thinkers like Aristotle or Einstein always challenged the predominate view. Aristotle proved that intelligence is not equal to nobility, by teaching a slave boy math, and Einstein won a Nobel Prize

---

13. As was discovered by the makers of Baby Einstein's that watching educational material is counterproductive to speech and brain development

by being a patent clerk and a high school dropout. Each persevered against all odds either from the anti-Semitism of Austria or the treachery of nobility in ancient Greece. We have become lulled into submission by the demagogues of modern culture, being glued to TV. Being obsessed about scandalous behavior of a Queen or the cheapness of beauty of a beauty queen.

Imagination is considered one of the loftiest gateways to G-d. It allows us to transcend physicality by diminishing it *'breaking unto the other side'*. Our sages understood, however, that the visual cortex of the brain allows for witchcraft and idol worship as much as it allows for prophecy. By redirecting the power of imagination Jewish Sages curved the potential for doing abomination which was so prevalent during Elijah's time until King Nebuchadnezzar's conquest and ultimate destruction of the first Temple. During the prophet Elijah's historic period there were some that were able to cause inanimate objects to talk and fool people into believing charlatans. Elijah was able to show the worthlessness of these magicians and preserve the Jewish Nation from a spiritual demise. There were many other Sages during different time periods that were able to manipulate nature in nondestructive ways because their interests did not lie on the path of self aggrandizement, but rather providing a clear passage of time for the Jewish Nation. Only those in total control of their sense of sensuality were able to understand the coded information that allowed them a prime line of communication to G-d, being able to see and understand more than a prophet.

Clearly, inventiveness has played a major role in the history of humanity. Like most things, it has the potential for ill or good, to draw us nearer to our Creator, or to drive us further into the shadows of mediocrity and evil.

DEVELOPMENT

THE PROGRESS ASSOCIATED WITH the active learning process is enhanced by culture's basic tenets that allow an infant to become a child. The basic events that go on in the family at this rudimentary stage make the infant acculturated and well attuned to the subtleties of any specific culture. This specific process is responsible for much of the information acquired throughout generations, or on an individual level, to further assimilate. The cultural basis becomes as ingrained as one's name, making up one's identity, full and rich of imagery of the inner wellspring of that way of life. They are absorbed by way of analyzing and by referencing different imagery and nuances. This child becomes well adjusted to his specific culture and society. Complex concepts are initially encountered as simple names or special symbols or festivals. He begins building ever so slowly a frame of reference to which adults have so much meaning. In Sparta a child of three would start using play swords, honor and duty become part of his nature. For a Jewish child, however, dressing up as Hommon or Ester, prayer and good deeds become part of existence. Children begin to absorb and imbue positive messages presented to them as objects, and sometimes parents through sheer ineptness begin to triangulate messages to one another ingraining bad character traits to their offspring as their parents did to them. Complexity of societal concepts and misnomers begin to settle into sub-consciousness, some take in Sukah is a booth where one eats, Purim is where one dresses up in a carnival type of atmosphere. Others take in boogeyman nightmares and perhaps even more seditious concepts.

The deeper meanings of all of those elementary aspects of religion come much later on but the identifiers and pseudonyms are already set in place. For example, the name Jacob – referring to our forefather in our culture – has profound meaning to it: Jacob was the founder of duality; he had the tenacious ability to possess, and to control the abundant gifts of wealth, and materialism that belonged to him while at the same time, having the capacity to imbue it all with altruism and spirituality, thereby enhancing his wholesome connection to the Divine.

Jacob is a role model for the rest of us who live out our lives combining spiritual and physical aspects while trying not to be inclined to either of the extremes and utilizing the Divine gift of time to its fullest. Similarly, one could refer to him as being the father of the twelve sons who later became the twelve tribes – the basis for our unifying Jewish identity until the present time. That identity has preserved us throughout millenniums, sustaining us, and making us unique in others' eyes; we are still here as a unified group, while others have long taken up their places on museum shelves, obviously having utilized time very differently.

This fusion of associative thinking and all of the processes involved in this synthesis of data is discussed in Jewish thought at great length. The actions and senses that are associated with it are essentially a communication of ideas through speech. Even books that also can facilitate this process of associative thinking are essentially a form of written speech. Thus communication and conceptualization of ideas always occurs through speech - G-d's gift to man. Through this Divine gift of speech, 'the living spirit', which is equated by our sages to a concept that includes cognitive, associative and many other processes that function inside the brain to produce a mature thought that via the use of the mouth becomes speech, is not only heard but reciprocated with a converse thought process.

ACQUIRING THE OUTSIDE WORLD

I N THE SAME PATTERN of thinking, known scientifically as associative synthesis, one can explain neural cell transmission, the igniting of different abstractions of information - building blocks in the inner tapestry of the mind where its intricate structures are being built, and are able to take in more and more information at a faster pace, formulating and building those inner towers of wisdom. These towers can be searched instantaneously as a thought is attempting to associate or differentiate one object from the multitude of similar ones, be it facts, human faces or concepts. Once the thought process is finished with the search, it reshuffles the tidbit into a suitable location and appropriately correlates with other facts and ideas of similar nature. It slowly builds larger images of the understanding of the inner building blocks that make up our world of understanding.

We can utilize these building blocks to construct an even larger and more refined image of the wisdom that is present around us and that G d has designed and placed in its proper position in the hierarchy of Creation. According to Jewish thought, each individual creation has many different 'wisdoms' that govern their capabilities, their designations, and potentials. Similarly, besides the physical makeup that is attributed purely to the complexity of the DNA structure of that object, our mature multifaceted minds have a purpose of destiny, that of giving to and sharing with others.

The biochemical process of 'firing neural cells', as it is known scientifically, is greatly concentrated upon in Jewish Mystic writings. Our Rabbis compare the focal time when a thought is being born or fired from one part of the lobe to the other to the process of the conception of a child. Initially it occurs in a vacuum of time, instantly materializing, then it begins to go through a metamorphosis of growth and concep-tualization, reshaped until full development, and made ready to be heard. Channeled to the vocal chords that in turn begin to open up the "double gated doors" [14]as the mouth and the moving of the lips, or shaping of the voice, are identified. The mouth and the lips are "**vessels**" that carry information of the "Divine soul" in the hands of its possessor. By this, we mean the actual act of germinating a thought or noticing that specific crucial point that creates and picks a correct solu-tion from an ostensible clutter of facts. That initial clutter of thoughts is constantly being analyzed by the deductive reasoning, eliminating unmatched or wrong conclusions to arrive at the correct answer. It is not defined as a vessel, but rather, as a seed. The allegory is that what one reaps is what one sows - good thoughts bring about good actions and rela-tionships, but bad ones only bring disaster.

The genesis of thoughts is a complex and fascinating topic.

---

14. Proverbs 13,3

The intense possibilities of human thought is part of what separates humanity from all of the Earth's other creatures. This subject has been at the forefront of Jewish religious thinking for centuries, and scientists are of course quite interested as well.

THE ESSENCE OF TIME
AS A DISCOVERY

THE SUPPORTERS OF AI (Artificial intelligence) claim that heuristics[38] is a major cornerstone to their programming techniques. Their claim stems from the basic understanding of how a thought[39] process occurs. Same as a baby learns how to walk through trial and error constantly learning from the mistakes of falling and not keeping balance, similarly they postulate that their technique of keeping history of successful resolutions[40] to any request capable of thinking ahead[41]. However, no AI program was able to come up to the level of complex human decision making, rather rudimentary guessing or sophisticated prognosticating. There is even a dispute amongst developmental psychologists as to what exactly is heuristics and is it pertinent to describe the complexity of the thought process. Their conclusions stem from a Darwinian assumption that mankind originated from some sort of primate roughly 12,00015 years ago. However, there is no scientific evidence or any kind of archeological

---

15. Latest findings and DNA evidence shows little correlation to Neanderthal, who apparently didn't even have the capacity to talk; not even humanoids of 50,000 years ago come close to societal sophistication of humans of even 8,000 ago. The earliest remains of those who started building cities or domesticating livestock or agrarian practices by actively planting and reaping wheat harvests can only be accounted for no earlier than 5,800 years ago.

discovery that can substantiate their claim. Their heuristic concepts can't accommodate the "reflex" that any doctor can demonstrate by a newborn moving their legs in a sequence of walking. It is true that the more intelligent person has a faster memory response and therefore higher capacity in resolving any IQ puzzle that is used to measure human IQ. Further, the deductive reasoning that Einstein had demonstrated can't be matched to any kind of economics prognostications of the most successful economists. Implying that heuristics with which Einstein was able to deduce his equations is dissimilar to any other human genius and any one's heuristic level is highly dissimilar to any one else's. The moment of discovery is when thought reaches an impasse and then comes a sudden heuristic jump that did not seem to arise from deductive process. This pivotal step, cathartic in nature, is the most blissful because it brings a solution or a discovery. The moment of discovery is when a thought reaches an impasse and then comes to a sudden heuristic jump that did not seem to arise from deductive process. This pivotal step, cathartic in nature, is the most blissful because it brings a solution or a finding. This sudden discovery - formation of the seed - is compared to the creation of something out of nothingness, or "totality of blackness" as it is referred to in the mystic texts. Our Sages consider that pivotal second as something that is beyond time, unbound by physicality, emanating from the Divine and giving our souls sustenance. It is reached through a struggle within oneself, not being obtuse and selfish, but relying on something higher. Those who have a tighter connection to G-d learn these heuristic steps or are given them throughout the learning process as a heavenly gift for their pure devotion to G-d. This potential is open to all human beings, yet the inclination of one's heart and mind will determine to what extent any individual is capable of acquiring such discernment.

SELFISHNESS

IN THE COURSE OF the deductive process of comparing similar events or resolutions of life's events, we dig up those dormant memories that are not as pleasing as others and are perhaps even egotistic in nature but are important for constant growth. As humans, it is only natural to transgress. But by recognizing and regretting the painful outcome of our transgressions, we tend not to repeat the same mistakes again, and can compare ourselves to graduating to an elevated grade. The family represents a constant learning process; it begins with "Mommy and Teddy Bear" and then becomes more complex — involving parents, brothers and sisters. Later on, the lessons transcend to viewing how the older generations are treated – either with reverence or the lack of it.

All of this training evolves around time, the gift for purposeful living. With their behavior patterns, parents begin, inadvertently, to teach their children respect, duty, honor, giving, caring and most importantly–sharing. Sometimes, for the first time in our lives, we, parents, begin to realize how important some of those things are, since we have such demanding pupils, our children, who will, one day, play the same role towards us as we to our parents[16]. This constant balance between learning and teaching forces us into becoming better caretakers, and evolves into a cornerstone for the maturity that only comes with those situations involving children, family and other obligations that do not allow us to be selfish.

The learning curve in this maturation process can, indeed, be made easier and less painful if one just begins to recognize others around oneself: friends, neighbors, animals and even trees - all that have some sort of feelings and desire to survive and do not have to come into conflict with us. In truth, our inner beings actually desire others' companionship and not their isolation from us. And, sometimes, by being selfish and looking out merely for 'what is in it for me', one dissociates oneself from that social interaction that is so important for inner growth and that ultimately results in detriment for oneself.

The lessons gleaned from the raw outcome of being selfish are sometimes very bitter to swallow if we never picked them up as children. Most importantly, when we are self-absorbed and selfish, we drive away any possibility of beneficial social company. Those that are selfish usually begin to attract those who, ironically, seek comfort and attention; they are willing to even take abuse in exchange for it and oftentimes reciprocate the selfishness in doses. These lessons are crucial for any viable future, yet are the toughest lessons one will ever acquire.

---

16. Proverbs 13,1

G-d spurs this catharsis in each of us in order to cause maturity. The very same concept of a living soul – speech - which is given to mankind for the purpose of becoming complete and not just babbling ideas around, was not given to some of the earlier creations, such as certain types of angels. These angels do not have the opportunity to become greater, closer to the Creator, and to receive His presence with awe and complete adoration while having the direct channeling of energy that sustains all of His creations. This "living soul" sustains us, if we only allow it to do so without animalistic desires getting in the way. With this gift, G-d gave us the opportunity to become greater than angels. Like any gift, of course, it can be either gratefully accepted, or rejected and thrown away.

THE LIVING SOUL

THE NEUROSCIENTISTS CLAIM THAT souls don't really exist and that they are merely a human invention. They further propose that our dreams are just thoughts that have not been resolved during the day, attempting to be resolved. In their perception the brain is just a giant neural network of millions of processors which are constantly busy revising or searching, controlling different muscle groups. They are busy proving and disproving theories based upon certain inconclusive ideas: the left cortex is more artistic and the other one is more cerebral, for example. But soul does not fit anywhere in this scheme[42]. It is true that complex interactions in the brain cause a person to become more agile or think faster or become responsive to different environmental stimuli. Examples would be a lecture where the brain needs to concentrate and to remember; or during a concert, which produces relaxation; or when driving one needs to be more alert and reactive to driving conditions and bad drivers. But do these physical processes in and of themselves adequately explain human consciousness? Or is this view missing a huge part of the overall big picture?

The Jewish view offers a much more multidimensional perspective, seeing body and soul as one, and emphasizing psychosomatic unity. Sages say that human eyes are a portal to the soul. When a person sleeps his body goes into a death of some sort where only 1/60 of the body functions. Some dreams are direct messages that G-d is sending to some as answers, which are then translated based upon that individual's sensory database. The soul itself consists of 5 parts, where the first one deals with here and now, but the highest one uniquely positions itself in the real world of the Creator where there is no time or space. Some people's souls are so attuned to spirituality that their fifth part is communicating to the lower parts being in a continuous connection to the Divine. This perception introduces the view, not that I have a soul, but that I *am* a living soul - a soul that is hooked into something else, but that I am a living soul, a living being.

Then we've got to ask, "Well, okay, what is it that is distinctive about this kind of soulishness?" What I want to suggest is that one of the central concepts of soulishness is the idea of relatedness: relatedness to others, relatedness to self, and, above all, relatedness to God. The living soul struggles within each one of us to improve, to become better and greater, causing our animalistic side to be uplifted through the usage of time. Through this constant battle, with the essence of life being at stake, and so much to gain, we still tend to take the more traveled roadway of the sinners - either because it is easier or because the other more altruistic path seems alien. The altruistic path is of piousness and constant self-sacrifice, and it is accompanied with a great deal of fulfillment and reward. For someone unfamiliar with this 'right' road, it seems less secure. Although one can feel temporarily grounded by taking this route through life's evolvement, in reality, it is as if one climbs a grand mountain for the possibility to gain a better perspective on all of his surroundings. The reward for conquering the mountain of one's animalistic selfish tendencies is extremely great and brings one closer to G-d.

With every step on the "right" route, G-d becomes even closer, more obvious, and less hidden by physicality; the element of time becomes more divine. That central transformation that sometimes occurs when inner change takes place brings an inner-soul freshness, invigorating the body, as if a newborn has just appeared. It germinates that superior seed, and allows it to grow and become a forest of comfort and tranquility.

There are those of the opinion that time gives us an opportunity to make an audit of sorts. We take stock of all of our actions, as if with a balance sheet that we carry within ourselves that at the end of the year becomes poignant and very palpable. Then at the end of days, on the deathbeds - during the transition into the next existence - we are forced to take stock of our inventory, and see where and in whose company we will be placed. When the final scorecard will be tallied, all will be accountable for their actions and the results that they brought upon themselves and others because of those actions. For example, Hitler will be judged for all of those lives that he snuffed out and for all of those future generations that did not have an opportunity to come forth and make a mark on reality. Conversely, a scholar like Maimonides will be given credit for his work that has influenced countless generations.

According to our Sages in the Bible, acts – even seemingly small ones – that impact life in a positive sense and do not allow time to slip away, are likened to the 'giving of life' and not death. Our Sages further explain that each point in life is a pivotal point for some other event that did not transpire yet. Every action has a ripple effect in time in one's own life or in the life of others. Some of these ripple effects become known as a conclusion. Those moments might seem harsh upon occurrence, but in reality, they may very well be the "cure" for the coming ensuing "illness."

We of course, when punished, do not see any benefit and begin to scream in panic and wonder "Why? Why? Why?" We plead for mercy and perhaps become reawakened to our misdeeds or to life and the One who grants it. Similarly, from a historic perspective, G-d creates a cure for the devastation that awaits us at every step of the Jewish endurance. Thus, He brings hope and salvation for the next generation that hopefully learned from their forefathers' mistakes. A similar process may be developing within on an individual level as well. Sometimes G-d takes us on a long circular way, bringing us back to the starting position, in order for mistakes to be rectified. This can be brought about by a painful lesson or memory that reminds us to be vigilant upon similar confrontations of challenge, allowing us to choose the right path and not fall into the same pitfalls of the past.

The more we learn of our Creator, the more we learn of ourselves. Life teaches us many lessons, but none of them will really be able to guide us into the truth until we recognize ourselves as the living souls that we're certainly created to be.

CONNECTION TO THE GODLY

IN OUR DAILY LIVES, we often analyze the events that come about. We react to them, compare them, and ultimately formulate an opinion or decision based upon them. Following this subconscious process, we choose whether or not we want to view and participate in the inevitable transpiring history that unfolds before us. This plan may contain many complex nuances that are only relevant to each one of us individually. On an individual level, G-d has predestined any specific event, or, perhaps, even the reaction that our inner being has to that event. This is because certain reactions are not called choices but instinctual behavior (i.e., some have an innate desire to give charity, while others feel no pull to do so). Doing these acts of caring we not only imitate the Creator and His ways in the physical world, but imbue our life with spirituality. In this course of behavior we establish a private connection to the Divine that each one of us experiences.

This tiny web of connections that we form with the Divine and allows us to stay on the correct course is reinforced with each and every desire to follow and perform His precepts willfully (there are 613 positive and negative precepts of G-d). By doing so, we are considered part of the Creator's Will, ultimately, becoming connected with the totality of the Will of the Divine by cleaving unto Him and totally abdicating our own selfish desires.

In reality, only certain mystics could attain this total suffusion of the Divine in their lives. It allowed them to transcend time and physicality, and to see the cause and effect as one direct stream that is not bound by time, and, perhaps, even to see events that were not yet born. The rest of us, who are not yet that attuned to the Will of the Divine, have to be bound to the meagerness of being blind to the characteristics of everyday events, while constantly struggling to choose the right path.

Our thinking process is composed of remembering and associating different facts and factors. However, it plays a minuscule role compared to that of accepting life as G-d gives it, and not letting it slip by. According to Jewish lore, based on the verse, "And He breathed a living soul," unlike a wind-up toy that comes to a standstill once it has used up all of its momentum, we become infused with vitality with each lesson that we learn through the span of our life years. Adam originally possessed an abundance of qualities. He could understand animals, their needs, and their wants. He was able to influence events by knowing their future outcomes, not only by thinking ahead and working all of the consequences, but with Divine intervention. He was able to change that which did not happen yet. We, as humankind, inherited these abilities but we only barely learn how to scratch the surface.

With the exception of the select few who played a role in the process of creation, the angels were not endowed with this gift of choice. Only certain special ones played a role in the process of creation. These angels were partners with G-d – and, therefore, are partners with us, as well, if we follow the right course. That 'breath of G-d' carries with it all of the substructures that allow us to communicate and relate to one another on a more sophisticated level, identifying similarities in ways of thinking, communicating and living a fulfilling life - unlike the animal kingdom where the survival of the fittest rules.

The conceptual problem arises when one has to consider the role of time –one of the initial building blocks of our universe - as a physical element that plays an essential part in humanity. With all of its significance and stature, time has no relevance to those very angels that were placed as guards over the physical elements of our external universe – or even, our internal universe.

As for man, we can acquire an internal growth that cannot be measured in inches or in weight. This growth is impalpable, yet with every measurement of that spiritual progress, we receive somewhat of a grander insight into the fabric of G-d's creation. The very nature of our own existence becomes daunting, bringing newer awakening into the ordinary, humdrum rhythm of the mundane manner in which we sometimes view G-d's gift of life. We are lulled into thinking that it is another passing glimpse of the sameness that from time to time becomes nauseating and boring, rendering us totally lost. Interestingly, those moments of boredom are the very precious instances that G-d bestows through His total kindness as a gift to be able to grow as people by inhaling a certain amount of His presence, and expanding our spiritual lungs, and ultimately allowing ourselves to become greater in front of the throne of His Majesty.

To complicate matters further, each uttered thought which falls on others' ears becomes an angel of sorts – a message with an address, force, purpose, and, most importantly, a destination. These specific man-made angels, or 'pearls of wisdom', have a way of reaching G-d, the originator of that power process in the first place.

These and many other types of angels that each and every one of us produces on a daily basis compound themselves into our own self-image in front of the 'Heavenly Throne'. The only reason why G-d has designed this aspect of time the way it is, is so that we, as humans, may have an opportunity to grow spiritually and become visible in front of His throne. We thereby become closer to Him – even perhaps reaching the very same spiritual location as those chosen angels who are partners to the Divine in the continued process of creation and completion of His work.

Every one of us has this potential to connect with both G-d and with our fellow human beings. Such a connection makes us keenly aware of the unique role that each of us has to play in this universe in which we live.

CONCLUSION

T HE ORIGINAL MAN'S PURPOSE was to be a gardener in the Garden of Life, giving shape to the bushes, making alleyways, beautifying the landscape and bestowing upon it greater glory. Perhaps for us, as his descendents, it is still our duty to make this world into Eden. With each piece of holy wisdom that we put out for public consumption, we uplift this world from its physicality and transform it into a loftier spirituality, bringing back the Garden to its rightful place. By doing so, we are the proud partners in G-d's master plan. By eliminating or curbing our physical desires and needs, we elevate our bodies and our surroundings. Our lives become worth living and have a Divine purpose.

This means we will be compelled to live a life that transcends the mundane and seeks to live in the beauty and glory that is imbued in the fabric of G-d's design.

APPENDIX

1   A **supernova** is a stellar explosion that creates an extremely luminous object. A supernova causes a burst of radiation that may briefly outshine its entire host galaxy before fading from view over several weeks or months. During this short interval, a supernova can radiate as much energy as the Sun would emit over 10 billion years. The explosion expels much or all of a star's material at a velocity of up to a tenth the speed of light, driving a shock wave into the surrounding interstellar medium. This shock wave sweeps up an expanding shell of gas and dust called a supernova remnant.

    Several types of supernovae exist that may be triggered in one of two ways, involving either turning off or suddenly turning on the production of energy through nuclear fusion. After the core of an aging massive star ceases to generate energy from nuclear fusion, it may undergo sudden gravitational collapse into a neutron star or black hole, releasing gravitational potential energy that heats and expels the star's outer layers. Alternatively, a white dwarf star may accumulate sufficient material from a stellar companion (usually through accretion, rarely via a merger) to raise its core temperature enough to ignite carbon fusion, at which point it undergoes runaway nuclear fusion, completely disrupting it.

2   A black hole is a region of space in which the gravitational field is so powerful that nothing can escape after having fallen past the event horizon. The name comes from the fact that even electromagnetic radiation (e.g. light) is unable to escape, rendering the interior invisible. However, black holes can be detected if they interact with matter *outside* the event horizon, for example by drawing in gas from an orbiting star. The gas spirals inward, heating up to very high temperatures and emitting large amounts of radiation in the process.

    While the idea of an object with gravity strong enough

to prevent light from escaping was proposed in the 18th century, black holes, as presently understood, are described by Einstein's theory of general relativity, developed in 1916. This theory predicts that when a large enough amount of mass is present within a sufficiently small region of space, all paths through space are warped inwards towards the center of the volume, forcing all matter and radiation to fall inward.

3   Every eleven years, our Sun goes through a solar cycle. A complete solar cycle has now been imaged by the sun-orbiting SOHO spacecraft. A solar cycle is caused by the changing magnetic field of the Sun, and varies from solar maximum, when sunspot, coronal mass ejection to solar minimum, when such activity is relatively infrequent. Solar minimums occurred in 1996 and 2007, while the last solar maximum occurred in 2001. This picture is composed of a SOHO image of the Sun in extreme ultraviolet light for each year of the last solar cycle, with images picked to illustrate the relative activity of the Sun.

4   Talmud hagiga 13, a Psalms 90
תהלים צ' ימי שנותינו בהם שבעים שנה

5   The concentration of Esoteric Hitlerism is on the Nazis' race-specific pre-Christian "pagan" (including Hindu) mythologies, and the inclusion of Adolf Hitler in the network of these mythologies.

The role played by mysticism in the development of Nazism and its ideals was identified by outsiders at least as early as 1940, with the publication of Lewis Spence's *Occult Causes of the Present War*. Incidentally , Spence accurately identified a pagan undercurrent in Nazism (for which he largely blamed Alfred Rosenberg), though some of his other conclusions - such as connecting Nazism to the Illuminati, and automatically equating paganism with "satanism" - are perhaps less credible.

The origin of the Aryan race, the Teutons generally, and the Germanic peoples specifically, the putative superiority of said Aryans over other races, and what they claimed were the unique circumstances of their origin, are all key concepts.

Various locations, such as Atlantis, Thule, Hyperborea,

Shambhala and others are suggested as the precise location of this original society of Übermenschen.

Another key belief is that this Herrenrasse (master race) had been weakened through interbreeding with those they thought of as *untermensch* or "lesser races".

6   **Nazism** developed several theories concerning **races**. They claimed to scientifically measure a strict hierarchy among "human races"; at the top was the "Nordic race", followed by lesser races. At the bottom of this hierarchy were "parasitic" races, or "*Untermenschen*" ("sub-humans"), which were perceived to be dangerous to society. Lowest of all in the Nazi racial policy were Africans, Gypsies and Jews. Gypsies and Jews were eventually deemed to be "*Lebensunwertes Leben*" ("Life unworthy of life"). Jews, and later Gypsies, became second-class citizens, expelled from Nazi Germany before being interned in concentration camps, then exterminated during the Holocaust (see Raul Hilberg's description of the various phases of the Holocaust). Richard Walther Darré, Reich Minister of Food and Agriculture from 1933 to 1942, popularized the expression "*Blut und Boden*" ("Blood and Soil"), one of the many terms of the Nazi glossary ideologically used to enforce popular racism in the German population

7   The Shah became a stalwart admirer of Hitler and the concept of the Aryan master race. He also sought the Nazis' help in reducing British petro-political domination. The Shah went on to rename his country "Iran" in 1935, which in Persian means 'Land of the Aryans' and refers to Airyanem Vaejah, the Avestan name of the original homeland of the Aryans. Although the land has been known as Persia to the native people themselves for many centuries.

The idea for the name change was suggested by Iran's ambassador to Germany, who came under the influence of Hitler's trusted banker Hjalmar Schacht (*Edwin Black, Banking on Baghdad*).From 1939 to 1941 Iran's top foreign trade partner (nearly 50% of its total trade) was Germany, which helped Iran open modern sea and air communications with the rest of the world.

8   "...On the 7th day of the Sukkot (Tabernacles) festival, the judgment of the nations of the world is finalized. Sentences are issued from the residence of the King. Judgements are aroused and executed on that day." (Zohar Vayikra - 31b)

9   On the 7th day of Sukkot, in the year 5707, corresponding to October 16th, 1946, the 10 aids to Hitler were hanged after being found guilty of crimes against humanity at the Nuremberg trials. Newsweek magazine (October 28, 1946, Foreign Affairs Section, page 46), ran a story on the hanging. Eleven were to be hung, but Goering, who was known to be a cross dresser, committed suicide in his cell shortly before the sentence was carried out. Perhaps suggesting the Homan's daughter who fell out of balcony.

10 In the story, Ahasuerus is married to Vashti, whom he puts aside after he asks her to appear "before the king with the crown royal, to show the people and the princes her beauty: for she was fair to look on", and she refuses. Mordecai's cousin Hadassah, also called Esther, is selected from the candidates to be Ahasuerus's new wife. The King's prime minister Haman (an Agagite) and Haman's wife Zeresh plot to have Ahasuerus kill all the Jews, without knowing that Esther is Jewish. Esther saves the day for her people: at the risk of endangering her own safety, she warns Ahasuerus of Haman's plot to kill all the Jews. Haman and his sons are hanged on the fifty cubit gallows he had had built for Mordecai, and Mordecai becomes prime minister in Haman's place. However, Ahasuerus's edict decreeing the murder of the Jews cannot be rescinded, so he issues another edict allowing the Jews to take up arms and fight to kill their enemies, which they do, killing 75,000 men, in addition to women and children.

11

אִישׁ	וְאֵת
פַּרְשַׁנְדָּתָא	וְאֵת
דַּלְפוֹן	וְאֵת
אַסְפָּתָא	וְאֵת
פּוֹרָתָא	וְאֵת
אֲדַלְיָא	וְאֵת
אֲרִידָתָא	וְאֵת
פַּרְמַשְׁתָּא	וְאֵת
אֲרִיסַי	וְאֵת
אֲרִידַי	וְאֵת
וַיְזָתָא	עֲשֶׂרֶת

12

Event	Dates
Ahasuerus ascends the throne of Persia	369 BCE
Ahasuerus's 180-day feast; Queen Vashti exiled, Queen Vashti was replaced by king Ahasuerus(according to christian Beliefs) (killed according to Jewish tradition)	366 BCE
Esther becomes queen	Tevet, 362 BCE
Haman casts lots to choose date for Jews' annihilation	Nissan, 357 BCE
Royal decree ordering killing of all Jews	Nissan 13, 357 BCE
Mordecai calls on Jews to repent; 3-day fast ordered by Esther	Nissan 14-16, 357 BCE
Esther goes to Ahasuerus; hosts First wine party with Ahasuerus and Haman	Nissan 16, 357 BCE
Esther's Second wine party; Haman's downfall and hanging	Nissan 17, 357 BCE

Second decree issued by Ahasuerus, empowering the Jews to defend themselves	Sivan 23, 357 BCE
Battles fought throughout the empire against those seeking to kill the Jews; Haman's ten sons killed	Adar 13, 356 BCE
Celebrations everywhere, except Shushan where second day of battles are fought	Adar 14, 356 BCE
Celebration in Shushan	Adar 15, 356 BCE
Megillah written by Esther and Mordecai; Festival of Purim instituted for all generations	355 BCE

13   Rebbe Nachman breathed new life into the Hasidic movement by combining the esoteric secrets of Judaism (the Kabbalah) with in-depth Torah scholarship. He attracted thousands of followers during his lifetime, and after his death, his followers continued to regard him as their Rebbe and did not appoint any successor. Rebbe Nachman's teachings continue to attract and inspire Jews the world over.

14   Sippurei Ma'asiyyot (Rabbi Nachman's Stories) (n.p., 1816)—13 seemingly simple "tales" in Hebrew and Yiddish that are filled with deep mystical secrets. The best-known of these tales is The Seven Beggars[1], which contains many kabalistic themes and hidden allusions.

15   **Shasu of Yahweh** is a term that appears in Egyptian inscriptions of the 18th and 19th Dynasties (c. 1540-1190 B.C.). One, found at Amarah or Amrah in Upper Nubia, dates to the reign of Seti I (c. 1300 B.C.). An earlier inscription, probably from the reign of Amenhotep III (c. 1400 B.C.) was found at the Temple of Amun in Soleb, Sudan. With time, however, it has generally become recognized for what it is. Redford states that "For half a century it has been generally admitted that we have here the tetragrammaton, the name

of the Israelite god, 'Yahweh'; and if this be the case, as it undoubtedly is, the passage constitutes a most precious indication of the whereabouts during the late fifteenth century B.C. of an enclave revering this god." Redford even goes so far as to call this group "nascent Israel."

16   An argument that they used that the account depicted in the Bible was a myth was the idea of camels being domesticated. The Patriarchs are described as having used camels for transportation. It was assumed that this was an anachronism. Camels were domesticated later, but of course the later people didn't know that their ancestors didn't have camels, and if they had camels they would of course have pictured their ancestors as having camels. Their great ancestors couldn't be less than they were.

17   For example, in 1960, the French translator Charles Virolleaud published a reading of a small, broken tablet known as KTU 1.96. The fuzzy photograph that accompanied his translation wasn't sufficiently clear to permit scholars to interpret the evidence from these ancient inscriptions for themselves. Virolleaud translated the first word as "Anat," who was a warrior goddess known from other Ugaritic texts. The text goes on to describe someone eating something. "So scholars thought the goddess Anat was a cannibal warrior [since] there's some anthropological literature about how if you eat somebody, then you ingest their power, becoming stronger, everyone has been writing about this aspect of the fascinating goddess Anat."

But the reading was wrong. Using a large-format, Lewis and his colleagues photographed the KTU fragment while in Damascus. "When we went back and analyzed the photograph, we found that the 't' of "Anat" isn't even there. "Just by correcting one letter, we've thrown out 37 years' worth of scholarship. So it shows the importance of getting the text read right," he said.

18   The price of **20 Shekels** which was paid for Joseph's slavery in Mesopotamia also affirms a relative date for Joseph in the *18th or 17th Century BC.* In his book, On the Reliability of the Old Testament, Kitchen writes:

"...the story of a young Joseph sold off [into slavery] into

Egypt fits in easily, especially in the early second millennium, in the overall period of the late Twelfth/Thirteenth and Hyksos Dynasties. After a good haggle, his brothers got 20 shekels for their young brother (Gen. 37:28). This we know to be approximately the right price in about the eighteenth century. This is the average price (expressed as one-third of a mina) in the laws of Hammurabi (§§116,214,252) and in real-life transactions at Mari (exactly) and in other Old Babylonian documents (within a 15- to 30-shekel range, averaging 22 shekels). Before this period slaves were cheaper, and after it, they steadily got dearer, as inflation did its work...After the eighteenth/seventeenth centuries, prices duly rose. In fifteenth-century Nuzi and fourteenth/thirteenth-century Ugarit, the average crept up to 30 shekels and more. (cf. replacement price of 30 shekels in Exod. 21:32.) Then in the first millennium, male slaves in Assyria fetched 50 to 60 shekels.

19 **Habiru** (Ha biru) or **Apiru** or **pr.w** (Egyptian) The Amarna letters written to Egyptian pharaohs in the 14th century BC) document a time of unrest in Canaan that goes back before the battle of Kadesh to the time of Thutmose I. Scholars pointed out similarities to Biblical accounts of Hebrews (i.e. `BRY (adj. form of the Hebrew 'Eber') putting people under the ban as they moved along the route of the kings highway through Edom and Moab into the territory of Ammon, Aram and the Amurru and realized that those records seemed to provide independent confirmation of the invasion of Canaan by Habiru fighting under Joshua, Saul, and David. Sources also discuss one Labayu, who had been an Egyptian vassal, and set up for himself. Attacking Megiddo, he assembled a group of Hapiru who consisted of both dispossessed local people and invaders. Having won Megiddo for himself, he gave his supporters Shechem for their own. (where descendents of Jethro lived)

An inscription on a statue found at Alalakh in southeastern Anatolia , the Mitanni prince Idrimi of Aleppo (who lived from about 1500 BCE to 1450 BCE), tells that, after his family had been forced to flee to Emar, he left them and joined the "Hapiru people" in "Ammija in the land of Canaan".

The Hapiru recognized him as the "son of their overlord"

and "gathered around him;" they are said to include "natives of Halab, of the country of Mukish, of the country **Nihi** and also warriors from the country Amae." After living among them for seven years, he led his Habiru warriors in a successful attack by sea on the city-state of Alalakh, where he became king.

The career of King Idrimi of Alalakh (*ca* 1500 – 1450) may provide a parallel on a grander social level: forced into exile, King Idrimi first fled to Emar on the Euphrates, and then to Canaan where he joined other Syrian refugees to live with the wandering Hapiru. His brief biography would not have appeared in inscriptions at all, if he had not been able to return and make a successful new bid for power in the city of Alalakah. When the Tell el-Amarna archives were translated, some scholars eagerly equated these Apiru with the Biblical Hebrews. Besides the similarity of their spellings, the description of the Apiru attacking cities in Canaan seemed to fit, loosely, the Biblical account of the conquest of that land by Hebrews under Joshua or even by names with David's Hebrew rally against Saul.

20 Abdi-Heba, the Egyptian vassal ruler of Jerusalem in the Amarna period (mid-1330s BCE), wrote a series of letters to the Egyptian king in which he complained about the activities of the "Habiru." The Hebrews were plundering the lands of the king. Abdi-Heba wanted to know why the king was letting them behave in this way; why was he not sending archers to protect his, the king's properties? If he did not send military help the whole land would fall to the Habiru.

21 A three-foot layer of ash, containing many pottery fragments and mud bricks from a wall, was found at the site, well preserved because it was sealed by sediments that accumulated over the years the destroyed city lay unoccupied. Excavations uncovered large quantities of grain stored in the ground floors of houses, indicating that the city fell shortly after the spring harvest. Buried stones, bricks and timbers were blackened from a citywide fire. The charred fragments have been dated at 1410 B.C., plus or minus 40 years. Finally, several Egyptian scarabs, or amulets, found in tombs at Jericho had inscriptions placing them in the same

period. Other evidence examined by Dr. Wood seemed to bolster the case for a Joshua connection.

22 Dr. Amos Nur, a Stanford University geophysicist, has written: "The combination, the destruction of Jericho and the stoppage of the Jordan, is so typical of earthquakes in this region that only little doubt can be left as to the reality of such events in Joshua's time."

23 The butterfly effect is a phrase that encapsulates the more technical notion of sensitive dependence on initial conditions in chaos theory. Small variations of the initial condition of a nonlinear dynamical system may produce large variations in the long term behavior of the system. So this is sometimes presented as esoteric behavior, but can be exhibited by very simple systems: for example, a ball placed at the crest of a hill might roll into any of several valleys depending on slight differences in initial position.

The phrase refers to the idea that a butterfly's wings might create tiny changes in the atmosphere that ultimately cause a tornado to appear (or prevent a tornado from appearing). The flapping wing represents a small change in the initial condition of the system, which causes a chain of events leading to large-scale phenomena. Had the butterfly not flapped its wings, the trajectory of the system might have been vastly different.

24 Calabi-Yau manifolds are important in superstring theory. In the most conventional superstring models, ten conjectural dimensions in string theory are supposed to come as four of which we are aware, carrying some kind of fibration with fiber dimension six. Compactification on Calabi-Yau n-folds are important because they leave some of the original supersymmetry unbroken. Essentially, Calabi-Yau manifolds are shapes that satisfy the requirement of space for the six "unseen" spatial dimensions of string theory, which may be smaller than our currently observable lengths as they have not yet been detected. A popular alternative known as large extra dimensions, which often occurs in braneworld models, is that the Calabi-Yau is large but we are confined to a small subset on which it

25   The pair encountered radio noise which they could not explain. It was far less energetic than the radiation given off by the Milky Way, and it was isotropic, so they assumed their instrument was subject to interference by terrestrial sources. They tried, and then rejected, the hypothesis that the radio noise emanated from New York City. An examination of the microwave horn antenna showed it was full of pigeon droppings (which Penzias described as "white dielectric material"). After the pair removed the guano buildup, and the pigeons were shot (each physicist says the other ordered the deed), the noise remained. Having rejected all sources of interference, the pair published a paper announcing their findings. This was later identified as the cosmic microwave background radiation (CMB), the radio remnant of the Big Bang. This allowed astronomers to confirm the Big Bang, and to correct many of their previous assumptions about it.

26   Measurements of the CMB have made the inflationary Big Bang theory the standard model of the earliest eras of the universe. The standard hot big bang model of the universe requires that the initial conditions for the universe are a Gaussian random field with a nearly scale invariant or Harrison-Zel'dovich spectrum. This is, for example, a prediction of the cosmic inflation model. This means that the initial state of the universe is random, but in a clearly specified way in which the amplitude of the primeval inhomogeneities is 10^{-5}. Therefore, meaningful statements about the inhomogeneities in the universe need to be statistical in nature. This leads to cosmic variance in which the uncertainties in the variance of the largest scale fluctuations observed in the universe are difficult to accurately compare to theory.

27   **String theory** is an as-yet incomplete mathematical approach to theoretical physics, whose building blocks are one-dimensional extended objects called strings, rather than the zero-dimensional point particles that form the basis for the standard model of particle physics. By replacing the point-like particles with strings, an apparently consistent quantum theory of gravity emerges, which has not been achievable under the standard model.

אני הצעיר יצחק דמן עכו ראיתי לכתוב סוד גדול שראוי להעלימו מאד. דע כי
יומו של הקב"ה אלף שנה שלנו שנ' כי אלף שנה בעיניך כיום. ושנתנו שס"ה
ימים ורביע יום. א"כ השנה של מעלה הם ג' מאות אלף שנה וחמשת אלפים
שנה ור"ן שנה שלנו. ושנתים של מעלה הם ז' מאות אלף שנה וכ"ה אלף ות"ק
שנים שלנו. מעתה צא וכפול צא וכפול עד ד מ"ט אלף שנה, שכל שנה ג' מאות
וס"ה יום ורביע יומת וכל יום של מעלה הוא אלף שנה שלנו כמ"ש ונשגב ה'
לבדו ביום ההוא מי ימלל גבורת ה'. בשכמל"ו. וכל זה כמש"ה אמנם ציורו
כפלי כפלים אלפי אלפי אלפים אינם בעיניו חשובים רגע. ויוצרו הוא צ"ע
(צדיק עליון). אמנם עם אין סוף די לך שתאמ' אין סוף.
וראיה ברורה על קיום העולם שנים רבות מאד שילאה הלב לחשוב אותם הוא
מאמר ישעיהו הנביא ע"ה שאאמ' הנער בן מאה שנה יומת שכשם שאנחנו
אומרים עכשיו על תינוק בן ג' שנים או בן פחותתינוק מת כן נאמ' לעתיד לבא
על איש שחי מאה שנה ומת תינוק מת לרוב השנים שיחיה אדם. ואם יבואו
קטני אמנה להכחיש ענין זר זה אומר לו ואשר להיות כבר היה שצתושלח חי
אלף שנה פחות ל' שנה. ודאי האיש אשר חי ק' שנה ומת בימיו של מתושלח
אמ' מתושלח עליו תינוק קטומת.
הנה עינינו רואות שקיום העולם ארוך מאד לחוציא מלבם של האומרים שאין
קיומו בלטי מ"ט אלף שנה שהם ז' שמיטות.

29   He contracted (in Hebrew "*tzimtzum*") Himself in the point
at the center, in the very center of His light. He restricted
that light, distancing it to the sides surrounding the central
point, so that there remained a void, a hollow empty space,
away from the central point... After this tzimtzum... He drew
down from the Or Ein Sof a single straight line [of light]
from His light surrounding [the void] from above to below
[into the void], and it chained down descending into that
void.... In the space of that void He emanated, created,
formed and made all the worlds (*Etz Chaim*, **Heichal A"K,
anaf 2**)

30   Albert Einstein a German-born theoretical physicist. He is
best known for his theory of relativity and specifically mass-
energy equivalence, $E = mc^2$. Einstein received the 1921 Nobel
Prize in Physics "for his services to Theoretical Physics, and
especially for his discovery of the law of the photoclectric
effect."

Einstein's many contributions to physics include his
special theory of relativity, which reconciled mechanics with
electromagnetism, and his general theory of relativity, which

extended the principle of relativity to non-uniform motion, creating a new theory of gravitation.

31   The concept of mass–energy equivalence unites the concepts of conservation of mass and conservation of energy, allowing rest mass to be converted to forms of active energy (such as kinetic energy, heat, or light) while still retaining mass. Conversely, active energy in the form of kinetic energy or radiation can be converted to particles which have rest mass. The total amount of mass/energy in a closed system (as seen by a single observer) remains constant because energy cannot be created or destroyed and, in all of its forms, trapped energy exhibits mass. In relativity, mass and energy are two forms of the same thing, and neither one appears without the other.

32   Greene was a prodigy in mathematics and rocket science. His skill in mathematics was such that by the time he was in sixth grade, he had to find a private tutor from Columbia University because he had surpassed his middle school's math level. His father, Alan Greene, was a one-time Broadway performer and high school dropout who later worked as a hunting coach. At Columbia, Greene is co-director of the University's Institute for Strings, Cosmology, and Astronomical Physics, and is leading a research program applying superstring theory to cosmological questions. He currently studies string cosmology, especially the imprints of trans-Planckian physics on the cosmic microwave background, and brane-gas cosmologies that could explain why the space around us has three large dimensions, expanding on the suggestion of a black hole electron, namely that the electron may be a black hole.

33   Flat space string theories are 26-dimensional in the bosonic case, while superstring and M-theories turn out to involve 10 or 11 dimensions for flat solutions. In bosonic string theories, the 26 dimensions come from the Polyakov equation. Starting from any dimension greater than four, it is necessary to consider how these are reduced to four dimensional space-time. A standard analogy for this is to consider multidimensional space as a garden hose. If the hose is viewed from a sufficient distance, it appears to have only one dimension,

its length. Indeed, think of a ball just small enough to enter the hose. Throwing such a ball inside the hose, the ball would move more or less in one dimension; in any experiment we make by throwing such balls in the hose, the only important movement will be one-dimensional, that is, along the hose. However, as one approaches the hose, one discovers that it contains a second dimension, its circumference. Thus, an ant crawling inside it would move in two dimensions (and a fly flying in it would move in three dimensions). This "extra dimension" is only visible within a relatively close range to the hose, or if one "throws in" small enough objects.

34

מדרש תהלים (בובר) מזמור צ ד"ה [ויב] תשב אנוש

תשב אנוש עד דכא ותאמר שובו בני אדם. אמר ר' אבהו בר זעירא גדולה תשובה שקדמה לבריאת עולם, ומה
היתה התשובה, היתה בת קול שמכרזת ואומרת שובו בני אדם. שבעה דברים קדמו לעולם אלפיים שנה, התורה,וכסא כבוד, וגן עדן, וגיהנם, ותשובה, והבית המקדש של מעלה, ושם משיח, ואנה היתה התורה כתובה, באש שחורה על אש לבנה, ומונחת על ברכו של הקב"ה, והקב"ה יושב על כסא הכבוד, וכסא הכבד מתוקן בחסדו של הקב"ה על הרקיע שעל ראשי החיות, אבל החיות לא היו באותה שעה, וגן עדן מימינו של הקב"ה, וגיהנם משמאלו,ובית המקדש מתוקן לפניו, ושם משיח חקוק על אבן יקרה על גבי המזבח, ובת קול מכרזת שובו בני אדם, והיו הכל נסבלין בכחו של הקב"ה, וכשברא הקב"ה את עולמו, וברא חיות הקדש, תיקן הרקיע עם כלם על קרני החיות,שנאמר דמות על (ראש החיות) [ראשי החיה] רקיע (יחזקאל א כב). אמר ר' הונא אמר ר' שמעון בן לקיש אלפיים שנה קדמו אלו עם התורה לברייתו של עולם, שנאמר ואהיה אצלו אמון ואהיה שעשועים יום יום (משלי ח ל), ויומו של הקב"ה אלף שנים, שנאמר כי אלף שנים (בעיניך כיום אתמול כי יעבור /תהלים צ'/ פסוק ד).

35   Psalms 104, He commanded to the world His Union (torah) to thousand generations.

36   In the 1950s and 1960s Sidney W. Fox, studied the spontaneous formation of peptide structures under conditions that might plausibly have existed early in Earth's history. He demonstrated that amino acids could spontaneously form small peptides. These amino acids and small peptides could be encouraged to form closed spherical membranes, called microspheres.

37   Did Homo erectus talk? Probably not, concludes anthropologist Ann MacLarnon. There's a major difference between

erectus and sapiens in the thoracic region. The vertebral canal in Homo sapiens is twice as wide as it is in erectus. Homo erectus is physically closer to an ape than it is to modern humans. And that is a distinction of considerable importance.

According to Ms. MacLarnon, erectus probably lacked the number of cell bodies which we have in our spinal chord. That means erectus had less muscle control in his rib section. Those muscles along with their supporting nerves control breathing. Finely controlled breathing is an essential requirement for speech. Apparently, erectus could not talk.

Apart from this anatomical evidence, we have another common sense reason for doubting erectus' ability to speak. If they were discussing and comparing their stone techniques, that should be enough to spark an occasional improvement over a million years or so. But we don't find any.

In many ways erectus seems almost like us. But something is missing. The cultural traits of language, funerary rites, and art are all absent. And as Johanson points out, "There is the troubling matter of a tool industry that didn't change for a million years.

38   In computer science, a **heuristic algorithm** is an algorithm that gives up finding the optimal solution for an improvement in run time. Two fundamental goals in computer science are finding algorithms with provably good run times and with provably good or optimal solution quality. A **heuristic** is an algorithm that abandons one or both of these goals; for example, it usually finds pretty good solutions, but there is no proof the solutions could not get arbitrarily bad; or it usually runs reasonably quickly, but there is no argument that this will always be the case.

For instance, say you are packing odd-shaped items into a box. Finding a perfect solution is a hard problem: there is essentially no way to do it without trying every possible way of packing them. What most people do, then, is "put the largest items in first, then fit the smaller items into the spaces left around them." This will not necessarily be perfect packing, but it will usually give a packing that is pretty good.

39   In psychology, a mental heuristic, or rule of thumb in which current behavior is judged to be correct based on how

similar it is to past behavior and its outcomes. Individuals assume that the circumstances underlying the past behavior still hold true for the present situation and that the past behavior thus can be correctly applied to the new situation. The **representativeness heuristic** is a heuristic wherein commonality between objects of similar appearance is assumed. While often very useful in everyday life, it can also result in neglect of relevant base rates and other errors.

40 In AI programming languages like prolog or lisp provides a method of searching for a similar or dissimilar correlations in data. It involves storing the steps that during previous execution lead to success attempting to simulate in the currant run to produce a positive outcome constantly storing previous steps, learning and improving. Heuristic increases the likelihood that person will repeatedly come to similar conclusion based on similar situation. This method simulates human habits and behaviors in routine situations.

41 The **contagion heuristic** is a psychological heuristic leading people to avoid contact with people or objects viewed as "contaminated" by previous contact with someone or something viewed as bad (or, less often, to seek contact with objects that have been in contact with people or things considered good). For example, we tend to view food that has touched the ground as contaminated by the ground, and therefore unfit to eat, or we view a person who has touched a diseased person as likely to carry the disease (regardless of the actual contiguousness of the disease).

   The contagion heuristic includes "magical thinking", such as viewing a sweater worn by Adolf Hitler as bearing his negative essence and capable of transmitting it to another wearer. The perception of essence-transfer extends to rituals to purify items viewed as spiritually contaminated, such as having Mother Theresa wear Hitler's sweater to counteract his essence.

42 The current view of psychiatry is that there are certain neurotransmitters that effect mood and so on. According to the evidence, 5-HT (**Serotonin**) is thought to be released from serotonergic varicosities into the extra neuronal space. Once this molecular substance is released into synapses it

begins to interact with other parts of the brain activating or deactivating proper responses. Which then begins to assemble different amino acids which are then deposited into the bloodstream to produce certain moods or cause extra sugars (glucose) to be released and cause different glands to produce needed response.

www.ingramcontent.com/pod-product-compliance
Lightning Source LLC
Chambersburg PA
CBHW072009040426
42447CB00009B/1549